# ABU DHABI
## GARDEN CITY OF THE GULF

Peter Hellyer and Ian Fairservice

MOTIVATE
PUBLISHING

Published by
# Motivate Publishing

**Dubai:** PO Box 2331, Dubai, UAE
Tel: (+971 4) 282 4060, fax: (+971 4) 282 4436
e-mail: books@motivate.co.ae   www.booksarabia.com

**Abu Dhabi:** PO Box 43072, Abu Dhabi, UAE
Tel: (+971 2) 627 1666, fax: (+971 2) 627 1566

**London:** 4 Middle Street, London EC1A 7NQ
e-mail: motivateuk@motivate.co.ae

**Directors:**
Obaid Humaid Al Tayer and Ian Fairservice

Written by Peter Hellyer and Ian Fairservice.
This edition edited by Jackie Nel and David Steele,
assisted by Zelda Pinto, with design by Johnson Machado

First published 1988
Second edition 1990
Third edition 1992
Reprinted 1994
Reprinted 1995
Fourth edition 1999
This edition 2003

© Motivate Publishing 1992, 1999, 2003

ISBN 1 86063 136 3

British Library Cataloguing-in-Publication Data. A catalogue record for this
book is available from the British Library.

Printed by Emirates Printing Press, Dubai

**His Highness Sheikh Zayed bin Sultan Al Nahyan**
President of the United Arab Emirates and Ruler of Abu Dhabi

# Foreword

IT IS MY PLEASURE TO INTRODUCE THIS NEW AND UPDATED edition of *Abu Dhabi – Garden City of the Gulf*.

Like its previous version, this edition presents an interesting portrait of the city of Abu Dhabi. It is a story of the place and its people that captures the important features of the city's history, character and achievements.

The pride that the people have in their city is clearly evident. I am pleased to note that this book presents a record of the progress made by the people of Abu Dhabi and their leaders. It is the people and their leaders who make history, and here in Abu Dhabi, history has been made on a grand scale.

Since the early 1970s, Abu Dhabi has experienced phenomenal growth due to the vision and hard work of His Highness President Sheikh Zayed bin Sultan Al Nahyan. Today the city stands as a model of success and progress. As we watch Abu Dhabi grow into one of the most important cultural and economic centres in the Middle East, we all share in the keen awareness of what this wonderful city has come to represent in its unique blend of modernity, history and heritage.

I take this opportunity to reiterate my view that our history and heritage is more than a series of events deemed important from the perspective of the present day. Instead, it's a progression of knowledge, beliefs and accomplishments from generation to generation and embodies the individual and collective wisdom of all those who have lived in this land. And, if our past, our present and our heritage are any indication of our future, Abu Dhabi will continue to reflect the unique spirit that has guided its development over the years. All of us who live and work in Abu Dhabi are proud to be part of that spirit.

**Sheikh Nahayan bin Mabarak Al Nahayan**
**Minister of Higher Education and Scientific Research**
**United Arab Emirates**

# Contents

## Chapter One

# The United Arab Emirates

In March 1968, the rulers of seven sheikhdoms known as the Trucial States, on the southeastern flank of the Arabian Peninsula, came together to form a federation. In the nature of such moves, it took a little while before the structure of the new state was finally agreed on but, on December 2, 1971, a new country, the United Arab Emirates (UAE), took its place on the international stage.

Emerging after a British presence in the region that had lasted a century and a half, the seven were disparate in size, population and resources, the smallest, Ajman, being a mere 259 square kilometres and the largest, Abu Dhabi, around 80,000 square kilometres. The total population in 1968 was only 180,000 and much of the country had no roads, no schools, no hospitals and little in the way of a modern developed infrastructure, even though the discovery of oil a few years earlier held out the hope of a brighter future.

The seven rulers, led by His Highness Sheikh Zayed bin Sultan Al Nahyan, Ruler of Abu Dhabi, felt they had little option but to agree to form a federation, for the British had made it clear that nothing would delay their departure at the end of 1971. With varying degrees of enthusiasm and confidence, the new state and its leaders set out to face the challenges of the future.

Many outside observers, citing poverty, history and the often tempestuous seas of Middle East politics, gave the new state little chance of success. As is so often the case, however, the foretellers of doom were proven wrong. In the years that followed, the United Arab Emirates underwent a rapid process of economic

*The famous Volcano Fountain is a colourful landmark in the heart of the city's commercial district.*

development and social change that occurred against a backdrop of enviable internal stability, despite the impact of two major wars and revolution in the region. This transformation was assisted by a mass immigration of expatriate workers that has seen the total population climb to more than 3.2 million.

The citizens of the UAE, which comprises the Emirates of Abu Dhabi, Dubai, Sharjah, Ra's al-Khaimah, Fujairah, Umm al-Qaiwain and Ajman, have seen their lives change totally within the space of a generation. Indeed, more than half of the country's citizens have been born since 1971, and have known nothing but federation. The speed of the transformation, and the way in which it has been absorbed, is particularly remarkable because the lifestyle of the people had remained almost unchanged for hundreds, perhaps thousands, of years – a life of unrelenting struggle to live in one of the world's most unyielding environments.

The old ways involved survival in the heat of summer in one of the most austere deserts on earth, on the edge of the Rub al-Khali (The Empty Quarter), or in the Hajar Mountains, where a brief respite during winter rains was soon forgotten amid the baked and barren rocks. Survival, on land at least, was a matter of pastoral nomadism or scratching a living from small agricultural plots, while the sea offered more in the way of resources, such as the world-famous pearls of the Gulf, although collecting them was a task to test even the most hardy.

Yet against this most uncompromising of backgrounds, the people of the Emirates have managed to survive, gaining their country an important place on the map of international maritime commerce, with Emirati sailors venturing to East Africa and China as far back as 2,000 years ago. Today, the UAE is one of the world's top oil producers and, thanks to the wealth from oil production and, more importantly, to the way in which the country's leaders have utilised that wealth for the benefit of the people, the hardships of the past are a fading memory.

While the people of the UAE continue to derive much of the strength of their society from the heritage of a difficult past, they are now able to look with confidence to a prosperous future.

## Abu Dhabi

The Emirate of Abu Dhabi, which has provided the overwhelming bulk of the funds that have paid for the federation's development, is by far the largest of the seven Emirates, with an area of 80,000 square kilometres, 17 times larger than the second-largest Emirate, Dubai, and amounting to more than 86 per

*Three generations of a Bedouin family photographed in 1971.*

*Modern Abu Dhabi is a cosmopolitan, high-rise city, but its foundations are firmly rooted in the Islamic faith.*

*Old traditions such as dance and music are still preserved at weddings and national festivals.*

cent of the total area of the federation.

It has the largest population, 1.18 million out of a total of 3.2 million, according to 2000 estimates, and also has the lion's share of the UAE's oil and gas resources. Though producing (in early 2002) some 1.8-million barrels a day, it has the capacity to produce half as much again, and sufficient reserves for more than 150 years at present production rates, as well as the world's fourth-largest reserves of natural gas.

Once a major power in southeastern Arabia (see chapter three, 'The land, its heritage and people'), Abu Dhabi fell on hard times in the 1930s and 40s, partially because of the international economic depression and the Second World War that followed, and partially because of the introduction of Japanese cultured pearls, which destroyed the market for Abu Dhabi's most prized export – the pure, natural Gulf pearl.

Ironically, oil, the source of the economic miracle that has since changed the face of Abu Dhabi and the other Emirates, was also first produced from beneath the sea.

Oil exploration in Abu Dhabi commenced in the late 1940s, although the first oil well, drilled at Ra's Sadr, northeast of Abu Dhabi, in 1950, was a dry hole. It was not until the late 1950s that commercially-viable oil deposits were found, first offshore at Umm Shaif, then onshore at Bab. Exports commenced in 1962 and Abu Dhabi entered the oil era. In 1966, a few years later, Sheikh Zayed became the Ruler of the Emirate and the process of development got fully under way. In the years that followed the Emirate was transformed and, thanks to the generosity of Sheikh Zayed, its oil revenues have also underpinned development elsewhere in the country.

The city of Abu Dhabi has, naturally, attracted a large proportion of the development expenditure, some of the results of which can be seen in the pages that follow. At the time that the production of oil began, it was little more than a coastal village and one which, moreover, appeared to have changed little in centuries, thanks to the economic slump that followed the collapse of the pearling industry.

A comparison between pictures from then and those of the city today show clearly the extent of the remarkable change. Amid the skyscrapers and broad thoroughfares of the city only three buildings from the past survive, one a simple watch-tower that still stands like a sentinel at the approaches to the island and another the old family fort of the ruling Al Nahyan family, more recently the Government's Centre for Documentation and Research and now destined to become a showpiece museum of the recent past. The third, not so easy to see, is a low, single-storey building that was once the summer residence of the Ruler. Built of coral and stone blocks, and roofed with mangrove poles, it lies just to the east of what was once Bateen Airport, at the inner end of the island. It is now scheduled to be incorporated in the new Khalifa Park being built in that area.

Abu Dhabi may lack some of the commercial vigour of its neighbour Dubai, but it does have the advantage not only of its oil revenues but also of massive financial reserves. In recent years, a move towards the privatisation of key sectors of the state-owned economy, coupled with an innovative offsets programme that requires companies that win major military contracts to invest part of the proceeds in productive industrial ventures, has stimulated industrial expansion and diversification.

At the same time, its dozens of parks, gardens and well-planted roadsides have given the city a green image that has, with justification, earned it the nickname 'Garden City of the Gulf'.

The Emirate of Abu Dhabi consists of much more than just the city itself. Roughly 160 kilometres east of the city lies its inland counterpart of Al Ain (itself the subject of another book in the Arabian Heritage Series: *Al Ain: Oasis City*). A conurbation of nearly a quarter of a million people, Al Ain is the heart of the Emirate's agricultural region, with farms and palm groves yielding tens of thousands of tonnes of produce a year, continuing an agricultural tradition that stretches back at least to the early Bronze Age, more than 5,000 years ago.

Southwest of Abu Dhabi is the Liwa Oasis, a small arc of oases on the edge of the Empty Quarter that is the traditional home of the Bani Yas tribal confederation, today headed by President Sheikh Zayed. To the north of Liwa is the burgeoning new township of Medinat (Bida) Zayed, capital of the Emirate's western region, which provides a good centre for touring the surrounding deserts, although the inexperienced should always take care when driving off-road.

The Emirate's coast begins at Ghantoot, in the northeast, running southwest past the huge Taweela power and water desalination plant and a sheltered system of lagoons and inshore islands that stretch to the capital, Abu Dhabi, itself an island, though with suburbs rapidly developing on the adjacent mainland.

To the west of the capital city lie more lagoons, islands and rocky headlands beyond the growing town of Mirfa, as far as the industrial complex of Ruwais and Jebel Dhanna, now an important centre for petrochemicals and oil refining, as well as the main oil export terminal. Furthest west of all is the vast expanse of the Sabkhat Matti, one of the largest salt flats in the world, with the barren and rocky Sila'a Peninsula on its western edge.

A fine highway runs just inland from the coast all

*A modern farm between the dunes near Al Ain oasis.*

the way from Ghantoot to Sila'a, a distance of more than 400 kilometres, with smaller roads or well-graded tracks permitting easy access to the coast at several points. Much more difficult to reach, however, are the Emirate's many islands. Some are little more than sandbanks, which may help to account for the fact that estimates of their number vary widely, but they certainly exceed 100.

Among the most important, apart from Abu Dhabi itself, are Abu al-Abyadh, the largest; Sir Bani Yas, now a nature reserve maintained by President Sheikh Zayed; Dalma, a centre of the fishing and pearling industries for thousands of years; Marawah, also with important archaeological sites; Qarnein, with breeding sea-bird colonies of international importance; and the oil industry islands of Das, Zirku and Arzanah. The varied geography and scenery will astound most visitors, but then the Emirate of Abu Dhabi, with its mix of modern development and traditional heritage, is in many ways a remarkable place.

*High-rise buildings provide a spectacular backdrop for traditional dhows moored along Dubai Creek.*

## Dubai

Second largest of the seven Emirates, Dubai has an area of 4,000 square kilometres facing on to the Arabian Gulf coast, with a desert hinterland and a small enclave at Hatta, on the road east through the Hajar Mountains to Oman's port of Sohar. Proud of its title 'Gateway to the Gulf' and its status as the uncontested commercial capital of the country, it has a history stretching back more than 4,000 years. The population in 2000 was estimated at 913,000, virtually all of whom live in the twin towns of Bur Dubai and Deira, the largest conurbation in the Emirates.

Ruled since 1990 by HH Sheikh Maktoum bin Rashid Al Maktoum, also the UAE's Vice-President and Prime Minister, Dubai has built upon its long heritage of trade astride the country's longest and deepest *khor* (creek), to dominate local commerce. With its ports of Port Rashid, in the city, and Jebel Ali, on the western edge, it handles nearly two thirds of the country's total imports, while a vast array of hotels and shopping, leisure and sports facilities has also contributed to its emergence as the top holiday

destination for visitors in the Arabian Gulf.

Although an oil producer, Dubai has relatively small reserves and has for many years recognised the need to diversify its economy in preparation for the day when the oil runs out, some time early this century. The diversification programme has achieved remarkable results. A sophisticated infrastructure has attracted hundreds of regional and international firms which use the city as their Middle East base.

Jebel Ali port, the largest man-made port in the world, is home to the region's largest free-trade zone, where more than a billion US dollars has been invested, and from where products are exported throughout the area. The requirement for a heavy industrial base has been met by companies such as the Dubal aluminium smelter and the Ducab cable plant, while assembly and manufacturing plants range from cars to computers.

In recent years, the focus has turned to hi-tech industry and the successful launch of Dubai Internet City and Dubai Media City has made the city a regional leader in modern communications and media technology.

More than 300 hotels, including world-class beach resorts, offer a wide choice of facilities for business and leisure visitors, while top international sporting events, such as the PGA Dubai Desert Classic golf tournament, the Dubai World Cup horse-race meeting, the Dubai Tennis Championships and world-championship powerboat racing, attract both the crowds and worldwide media attention.

Also home to one of the world's fastest-growing airlines, Emirates, the city is now able to attract more than a million visitors a year to events such as the annual Dubai Shopping Festival and the Dubai Summer Surprises. Cosmopolitan and free-wheeling in its approach to business, Dubai has successfully drawn on its commercial heritage to plan for the future.

## Sharjah and the northern Emirates

Stretching along the Arabian Gulf coast northeast of Dubai and away across the Hajar Mountains to the Gulf of Oman on the other side of the peninsula are the remaining five Emirates.

The largest of these is Sharjah, with an area of some 2,600 square kilometres and an estimated population of 520,000 in 2000. The city of Sharjah itself, a few kilometres north of Dubai, is the seat of the ruling Al Qasimi family, descendants of the sheikhs who battled the British for control of the waterways of the Arabian Gulf at the beginning of the 19th century. A branch of the family also rules the northernmost Emirate of Ra's al-Khaimah. Sharjah Emirate stretches inland to the oasis of Dhaid, in the lee of the Hajar Mountains, while there are three enclaves, Kalba, Khor Fakkan and Dibba al-Husn, on the coast of the Gulf of Oman.

Examples of Sharjah's ancient heritage can be found in the finely-restored forts and historic buildings in the old district of Sharjah city and in Kalba, as well as several archaeological sites. Tell Abraq, north of Sharjah, is a settlement mound dating back more than 4,000 years, while Muwailah, an Iron Age village near Sharjah Airport, has yielded the oldest writing ever found in the UAE, dating to the local Iron Age. At Jebel Buhays, south of Dhaid, archaeologists have found a Late Stone Age cemetery, more than 6,000 years old, with a mass grave of more than 200 people.

Sharjah prides itself on its cultural traditions. Indeed, the city was named by Unesco as 'Arab Cultural Capital for 1998', an honour much prized by the Ruler, HH Dr Sheikh Sultan bin Mohammed Al Qasimi, himself a historian of note. With several museums, an impressive cultural centre, Islamic-style architecture, two universities, the country's largest annual book fair and a lively tradition of art and theatre, the Emirate also lays uncontested claim to being the cultural capital of the UAE.

At the same time, it is rapidly developing a widely diversified economy. Oil and gas revenues from the offshore Mubarak field, and the Saja'a and Moveyeid fields onshore, have helped to underpin an industrial sector that focuses on light manufacturing.

The east coast port of Khor Fakkan is one of the UAE's top container terminals, capitalising on its strategic location outside the Strait of Hormuz to handle more than one million container units a year. The port of Hamriyyah, on the Arabian Gulf coast, is now an important terminal for the export of liquefied natural gas and condensate from the onshore oilfields.

Adjacent to the city of Sharjah is Ajman, smallest of the Emirates and surrounded on the land side by Sharjah, apart from two tiny mountain enclaves at Manama and Masfoot. Just 259 square kilometres in size, its population in 2000 was an estimated 174,000, many of whom work in Sharjah and Dubai but have been attracted by Ajman's competitive accommodation costs and less frenetic pace of life.

Deriving much of its income from the provision of services, Ajman has no commercially-viable deposits of hydrocarbons, but has successfully established one of the UAE's major heavy-industry ventures, the Arab Heavy Industries Shipyard, close to one of the UAE's major dhow-building yards. This offers visitors an interesting comparison of traditional and modern aspects of the country's long seafaring heritage.

Under the direction of its Ruler, HH Sheikh Humaid bin Rashid Al Nuaimi, the local Chamber of Commerce and Industry is pressing ahead with plans to attract more light manufacturing companies, which should help further diversify the local economy. The tourist industry, which has grown in recent years, is set to benefit soon from plans for an international airport that will cater primarily for business travel.

The next Emirate along the coast, Umm al-Qaiwain, is also developing industry, although more slowly. The main town, of the same name, as with all of the Emirates, sits on a peninsula that stretches out into the Arabian Gulf around 20 kilometres north of Ajman. With an area of 780 square kilometres, Umm al-Qaiwain has few resources. This is reflected in its population, the smallest in the seven Emirates with an estimated 46,000 inhabitants in 2000.

The desert hinterland of the Emirate, which is ruled by HH Sheikh Rashid bin Ahmed Al Mu'alla, stretches inland to the oasis of Falaj al-Mu'alla, although for most

visitors, the main attractions of Umm al-Qaiwain are its fine beaches, mangrove-fringed lagoons and the 2,000-year-old archaeological site at Ad Door. A small offshore gas field is set to come into production in 2003, linked to a supply grid for the whole of the northern Emirates. When it does, Umm al-Qaiwain will become the fifth Emirate to produce hydrocarbons.

The northernmost part of the UAE's Arabian Gulf coastline is occupied by Ra's al-Khaimah, whose Ruler, HH Sheikh Saqr bin Mohammed Al Qasimi, has been in power since 1948. With an area of 1,700 square kilometres and an estimated population in 2000 of 171,000, Ra's al-Khaimah is divided into two parts: one in the Hajar Mountains, near Hatta, and the other the bulk of the fertile Jiri Plain that stretches from Ra's al-Khaimah southwards towards the mineral spa town of Khatt and the village of Idhn.

Birthplace of one of the UAE's greatest figures, the 15th century navigator Ahmed bin Majid, Ra's al-Khaimah has long played an important role in the country's history, its ancient port of Julfar having traded as far away as China more than 1,000 years ago. It was also the naval stronghold of the Al Qawasim sheikhs in the 18th and early 19th centuries. Today, its economy is based primarily on agriculture, although

*Sharjah's Blue Souq offers a wide range of goods and is a major tourist attraction in the Emirate.*

a free zone is being developed north of Ra's al-Khaimah town. Looking to the future, however, the combination of fertile plains that can be as green as any African savannah after winter rains, and austere, rugged mountains offers considerable potential for the development of tourism.

All but one of the Emirates have their capital cities on the Arabian Gulf coast of the UAE. The exception is Fujairah, which lies on the Gulf of Oman coast, and whose population at the end of 2000 was estimated at 106,000. Its 1,300 square kilometres comprise a mixture of a fertile coastal strip, covered with farms and traditional date-palm groves, and a swathe of the Hajar Mountains. A small part of the Emirate lies on the western side of the mountains, between Habhab and Siji, the latter the home of a flower farm that's succeeded in finding a niche for its blooms in the highly competitive markets of Europe.

Ruled by HH Sheikh Hamad bin Mohammed Al Sharqi, Fujairah has maintained its traditional economic base of agriculture and fishing. At the same time, it has moved steadily and confidently in the development of a major container port. An oil-tank farm and refinery adjacent to the port reflect the Emirate's position as the third-largest marine

bunkering centre in the world, supplying millions of tonnes of fuel to thousands of passing ships every year.

The Fujairah Free Zone is the second largest in the country, with an investment worth more than one-billion dirhams, while at Qidfa the world's largest reverse-osmosis desalination plant is being built, which will supply power to the whole of the northern Emirates, as well as water to Al Ain.

Fujairah is a favourite weekend destination for residents of other parts of the UAE. Its attractions are mountain scenery, historic buildings (including a number of castles and forts), and long beaches, particularly in the northern strip between Dibba and Bidiya, site of the oldest mosque still in use in the country.

Fujairah is known as 'An Arabian Jewel' for the variety of its landscapes and it is now pinning part of its plans for development on the expansion of its tourism industry. In recent years, several new hotels have been opened, and more are being built, to cater for increasing numbers of visitors from home and abroad. These tourism developments complement other sectors of an already fast-diversifying economy.

## Chapter Two

# A man of his people

His Highness Sheikh Zayed bin Sultan Al Nahyan, President of the United Arab Emirates since its creation in 1971 and Ruler of Abu Dhabi since 1966, has guided his country through a process of peaceful development on an almost unparalleled scale.

The process involved a far-reaching vision that allowed him to see the possibility of changes that would be inconceivable to others, while carefully ensuring that the revenues from Abu Dhabi's oil production were used for the benefit of the country as a whole. Not surprisingly, he has come to be called the 'Father of the Nation'.

Sheikh Zayed has been actively involved in governing his people for more than half a century. Prior to becoming Ruler of Abu Dhabi, on August 6, 1966, he was for 20 years his brother Sheikh Shakhbut's choice as Ruler's Representative in the Eastern Region of the Emirate, based in Al Ain. Appointed to this post when still in his 20s, he gained experience in the mechanics of government and this stood him in good stead for future challenges.

The origins of his skills – and indeed of the vision that guided him in his tasks as Ruler's Representative, Ruler, and then, concurrently, as UAE President – lie further back, in a childhood and youth that provided him with an understanding of and love for his country and his people.

Sheikh Zayed was born around 1918 (the precise date is uncertain) to the wife of Sheikh Sultan bin Zayed, a younger brother of the Ruler of the day, Sheikh Hamdan bin Zayed. The last of four sons, he was named Zayed after his illustrious grandfather, Zayed bin Khalifa, who ruled Abu Dhabi from 1855 to

*HH Sheikh Zayed bin Sultan Al Nahyan.*

17

**Sheikh Zayed's philosophy of leadership, as with all else in his life, is based on his deeply held faith in Islam.**

1909, raising it to a position of pre-eminence in southeastern Arabia. Sheikh Sultan was but one of several brothers, and the Emirate of Abu Dhabi itself was far from prosperous, its main source of income, the international trade in pearls, having been brought virtually to a halt as a result of the First World War.

The young Zayed spent much of his boyhood in Al Ain, and it was here that he grew to manhood. During the years 1922 to 1924, when his father Sheikh Sultan was Ruler, he spent more time in the capital, Abu Dhabi, and continued to do so when his eldest brother, Sheikh Shakhbut bin Sultan, succeeded an uncle as Ruler in 1928.

There was little need for a mere stripling to be concerned with the often complex and contested affairs of state. Instead, Zayed stayed in Al Ain with his mother Sheikha Salama, taking full advantage of the scant opportunities available for education through a traditional Quranic school, and absorbing his knowledge of his family and their people from his relatives.

For much of the time he was to be found roaming the deserts and mountains, learning to shoot and hunt with falcons, a sport he still practises. He learned how to ride a camel, and how to identify where sweet water could be found under the sands, a skill that continues to surprise geophysicists and other scientists today. He also learned all he could about the people of the area, the semi-settled farmers of the oasis, and the nomadic Bedu of the desert, who visited for just a few months each year, bringing with them tales of tribal raids, distant wells and routes across the trackless sands.

His inquisitiveness was inexhaustible and, as the boy grew into a young man, he watched and listened as tribal elders sought to mediate and conciliate, learning the lesson that in a harsh environment the struggle for mere survival may be the toughest of all. Drinking deep of the traditions and heritage of his people, he came to develop an unshakeable belief in the religion of Islam, something that remains an essential part of his character today.

The young Zayed amassed a knowledge of the land which was to serve him well as he grew to manhood. He gained the respect and trust of the tribe, and patriarchs sagely compared the emerging leadership skills of Zayed with those of his grandfather.

As his reputation grew, so did the trust of his brother, Sheikh Shakhbut. When the first geological prospecting team obtained permission to journey through the sands of Abu Dhabi in the 1930s,

Sheikh Zayed, then still in his teens, was given the task of guiding them – a first encounter with the world of oil that was later to play such an important part in his life.

A few years later, he succeeded in mediating between two desert tribes whose age-old rivalries had broken out into open conflict, winning plaudits for his skills as a conciliator and mediator.

In 1946, a vacancy appeared for the post of Ruler's Representative in Al Ain. Despite his relative youth, Sheikh Zayed was the obvious choice to undertake the task for his brother. Wise beyond his years and well-versed in both desert lore and the ways of its people, he was already respected far beyond the borders of Abu Dhabi.

An early European visitor to Al Ain shortly after Sheikh Zayed took up his post was Edward Henderson, then working for Petroleum Development (Trucial Coast) at the beginning of a career in the region that was to span nearly five decades.

In his memoirs *An Arabian Destiny*, Henderson recalled the impression the young Zayed made upon him: "He was then around 30 years old," he wrote. "He was handsome, with humorous and intelligent eyes, of presence and bearing, simply dressed and clearly a man of action and resolution. Although he was young, and had been formally in charge of the Abu Dhabi section of the oasis and its surrounding deserts for only a brief period, he was experienced in the politics of the region, and was already by far the most prominent personality in the area. He had a sure touch with the Bedouin."

In the two decades that followed, refining his knowledge of the practice of governance as he went, Sheikh Zayed was to prove that the confidence shown in him by his brother was by no means misplaced. Under Zayed's leadership, Al Ain's development accelerated dramatically.

Al Ain had been a crossroads of desert trade routes for thousands of years, with evidence of human settlement dating back at least six or seven thousand years. At the same time, supplies of fresh water running off from the neighbouring Hajar Mountains made it a centre of agriculture, where crops such as wheat and sorghum have been grown since at least 2500 BC.

Recognising that one of his first tasks was to stimulate the local economy, Sheikh Zayed turned his mind swiftly to the revival of agriculture. After ordering the cleaning of the subterranean channels (the *aflaj*), he then ordered the construction of Falaj Al Sarouj, the first new system to be built in hundreds of years.

To ensure the *falaj* water was distributed as widely

*HH Sheikh Khalifa bin Zayed Al Nahyan,*
*Crown Prince of Abu Dhabi and Deputy*
*Supreme Commander of the UAE Armed Forces.*

and fairly as possible, he revised the old system of allocation and offered water free of charge to farmers. Formerly neglected land could now be irrigated, causing agricultural production to grow and, with it, the local economy. Al Ain soon began to resume its traditional position as a market centre for the entire inner desert region.

Casting a shrewd eye over the villages that made up Abu Dhabi's portion of the oasis, Sheikh Zayed went on to plan to integrate them into a larger town, and gave orders for the planting of trees along the edges of what were then simple sandy tracks. This was the beginning of the afforestation and planting that has today made Al Ain one of the greenest cities in Arabia.

As he settled into the task of governing Al Ain, Sheikh Zayed was exposed more and more to the outside world. By the late 1940s oil company officials such as Edward Henderson, and the explorer Sir Wilfred Thesiger, passed through and stayed with him. The Trucial Oman Scouts, a British-officered force set up at the beginning of the 1950s to keep the peace in the desert, established a camp at Al Ain in one of the traditional forts. From them, Sheikh Zayed

**Sheikh Zayed has always shown a great love for the children of the Emirates.**

learned more about the outside world and the changes taking place.

In 1953, he made his first trip overseas, accompanying his brother Sheikh Shakhbut to Paris and then going on to London. Amazed by the Eiffel Tower, he was more deeply impressed by the schools and hospitals he visited and decided that his own people should have access to similar facilities.

A few years after Sheikh Zayed had taken over as Ruler's Representative in Al Ain, the first oil well had been drilled in what was to become the United Arab Emirates, sparking the interest of oil companies, and others, from outside the Emirate.

With no clearly-defined territorial borders, the oasis centred on Al Ain was the focus of a dispute in the late 1940s and early 1950s, during which time Saudi Arabia laid claim to three villages, including Buraimi, which belonged to the Sultanate of Oman. Handling the dispute with dexterity along with old friends such as Edward Henderson – by now a British Government representative – Sheikh Zayed stood firm. In later years, after he had become Ruler of Abu Dhabi and then President of the UAE, he was to take the lead in working out an agreement that resolved the issue.

Such distractions, however, did not prevent Sheikh Zayed from devoting his attention to developing Al Ain. With its place as a regional market

re-established, he turned to improving the lot of the people in other ways. For example, he paid for the establishment of Al Ain's first modern school, also the first in the whole of the Emirate of Abu Dhabi, from his own private funds. Among early pupils were Sheikh Khalifa bin Zayed, his eldest son, now the Crown Prince of Abu Dhabi and Deputy Supreme Commander of the UAE Armed Forces, and Sheikh Surour bin Mohammed Al Nahyan, now Chamberlain of the UAE Presidential Court, as well as other members of the Al Nahyan family.

The discovery of oil in Abu Dhabi was not long delayed. After several unsuccessful attempts in the early 1950s, the search eventually paid off, with the discovery first of the Umm Shaif field offshore in 1958, then the Bab field onshore in 1960. The first cargo of Abu Dhabi's oil was exported in 1962. As the rising revenues flowed into the government's coffers, money became available for development.

Sheikh Zayed was determined to ensure that oil revenue was used to improve the lives of all the people of Abu Dhabi – a process that would involve an almost revolutionary change in their lifestyle. Rising expectations among the people, coupled with the fact that neighbouring countries were already advancing rapidly, meant that a choice for change was inevitable.

Sheikh Zayd was aware that the key to success lay

*In 1960, Murban (Bab)-3 was the first well to come on stream in the Emirate of Abu Dhabi.*

in ensuring that the change was brought about in a way that permitted the essential nature of society, its culture and traditions, to be preserved. This would provide a secure base on which the process of development could be anchored.

The wisdom of this approach and his already impressive record as a governor in Al Ain brought affection and respect at home, and attention from abroad. As British writer Clarence Mann wrote of him in 1964: "Sheikh Zayed is the principal authority (in Al Ain), and from here his influence stretches throughout Dhafra. He is highly respected by the Bedouin because he knows and practises their ways and traditions. It is through him that Abu Dhabi exerts its influence on the Bedouins, and this factor, plus his reputation for justice, advancement and statesmanship, would almost ensure that he would be chosen as his brother's successor."

On August 6, 1966, acknowledging the need for new leadership to meet the challenges facing Abu Dhabi, the Al Nahyan family chose Sheikh Zayed to take over the responsibilities of governing not only Al Ain, but the whole of the Emirate.

Sheikh Zayed had already developed a clear vision of how the process of progress should begin. After he became Ruler, he wasted no time in putting this vision into effect. Within a matter of weeks, a new structure of government was created and consultants were appointed to advise on roads, schools, hospitals, a port, an airport and all the other key components of the national infrastructure.

Inspecting projects himself, turning up unannounced to see what was happening, Sheikh Zayed instilled in others a determination to match his own that oil revenue should be used to build a new society.

Sheikh Zayed also faced the task of creating a new political structure for Abu Dhabi – one that would also involve its neighbours.

At the beginning of 1968, after a presence in the area that dated back to 1819, the British announced that they would withdraw by the end of 1971. Recognising that collaboration with the other six Emirates of the Trucial States was crucial, Sheikh Zayed agreed with the Ruler of Dubai, Sheikh Rashid bin Saeed Al Maktoum, to establish a federation, and invited the other five rulers to join.

By July 1971, agreement was reached, and the new United Arab Emirates (UAE) took its place on the international stage on December 2 of the same year, with Sheikh Zayed as President and Sheikh Rashid as Vice-President.

Looking back, more than 30 years later, the UAE has been a tremendous success. Despite the vicissitudes of the politics of the region, the UAE has grown to maturity as the most successful experiment in federation ever to take place in the Arab World.

Moreover, it has done so not merely in terms of political development, but also in the way the dramatic development has been successfully introduced to, and absorbed by, its people.

While Sheikh Zayed himself would be the first to say that the process owes much to the efforts of the rulers of the other six Emirates – his fellow members of the Supreme Council of Rulers – there is no doubt that without his wisdom and leadership it wouldn't have been possible, something his fellow rulers have themselves acknowledged by re-electing him to six successive five-year terms as President, most recently in December 2001.

The UAE has moved into a new phase of its history, and is facing the challenges of today and tomorrow with confidence.

The pace of development has been breathtaking. The population has grown from 180,000 to more than 3.2 million in little more than 30 years and

schools, hospitals, ports, airports, roads and other facilities cover the country as the revenues from oil production are directed into stimulating one of the world's fastest-growing economies.

On the international stage, Sheikh Zayed has won a reputation as a statesman of wisdom and patience, and a determined upholder of justice, so that the UAE has a far greater influence on the world scene than its size would suggest. Whatever his achievements as a statesman, Sheikh Zayed draws greater personal satisfaction from what he's been able to do for his own people.

Considering the changes in living standards since he was a boy, this is scarcely surprising. "Thank God that we've been able to achieve all that we sought to achieve for our people," he told one curious interviewer from the *New York Times* in early 1998. "At the outset, people questioned whether we'd be able to achieve our goals but, by the grace of God, we

*For nearly two centuries, Qasr Al Hosn was the Abu Dhabi home of the ruling Al Nahyan family.*

*A 1963 photograph of, from right, His Highness Sheikh Zayed; his brother the former Ruler Sheikh Shakhbut; and a third brother Sheikh Khaled. A fourth, Sheikh Hazza, had died in 1958.*

have achieved all that we sought, and more, beyond our most ambitious designs."

At one level, the achievement can be viewed in a purely material sense: the building of a modern infrastructure for what is, by any standards, a modern welfare state, where health and education are available for all, and where no-one need go to bed hungry. Much of that achievement can be seen elsewhere in this book.

At another level, the changes took place with the active support and involvement of the people of the Emirates. That a society whose traditions date back hundreds of years has absorbed and thrived on the changes is remarkable. It was made possible by the nature of the society itself, and the wisdom of Sheikh Zayed in ensuring its time-honoured foundations had been preserved and cherished.

As he told the *New York Times*: "Our method and style of government is based upon our religion and traditions, (and) it is what our people want. . . . We've always said that our people should voice their demands openly. We're all in the same boat, and they are both captain and crew. Our doors are open for any opinion to be expressed. . . .

"It's our deep conviction that God the Creator has created people free, and has prescribed that each individual must enjoy freedom of choice. . . . Those in a position of leadership should deal with their subjects with compassion and understanding, because this is the duty enjoined upon them by God the Almighty, who enjoins us to treat all living creatures with dignity. How can there be anything less for man, created as God's vice-gerent on earth?"

Sheikh Zayed's philosophy of leadership, as with all else in his life, is based on his deeply held faith in Islam. "It is Islam that asks every Muslim to respect every person," he told another interviewer. "Not, I emphasise, special people, but every person. In short, to treat every person, no matter what his creed or race, as a special soul is a mark of Islam. It is just such a point, embodied in Islam's tenets, that makes us proud of Islam. To be together, to trust each other as human beings, to behave as equals."

Looking back on more than 50 years in government, Sheikh Zayed can be well pleased at the changes he has seen, and for which, to a very large extent, he has been responsible, even though he would always share the credit with those who have worked with him.

Pomp and circumstance apart, leaving aside the praise often heaped on him, Sheikh Zayed remains a man both for and of his people.

## Chapter Three

# The land, its heritage and people

During the middle of the last century, Sir Wilfred Thesiger, the last of the great European explorers of the Arabian Peninsula, made his classic journey by camel from southern Oman across the wastes of the Rub al-Khali (the Empty Quarter), to the shores of the Arabian Gulf.

The story, as told in Thesiger's book *Arabian Sands*, is one of intense hardship as he and his Bedu companions struggled through the trackless, waterless deserts and across the high rolling dunes, urging their camels onwards to the water-holes and oases and to the Gulf beyond.

It is an epic story, too, of man's ability to survive in a land where nature itself seems determined to resist his presence.

Part of that journey lay within the Emirate of Abu Dhabi and Thesiger's descriptions of his arrival in the Liwa Oasis, and of his happy interlude hunting with Sheikh Zayed in the hinterland of Al Ain, are not only masterpieces of travel writing but also the best available descriptions in the English language of a now vanished way of life.

Unlike the other six Emirates that make up the UAE, Abu Dhabi is largely desert, with the dunes imperceptibly but relentlessly moving, year by year, across the land. For countless generations before Thesiger's arrival, the Bedu of the area had survived in the harsh conditions: although oil revenue has brought prosperity and development to the region, it is of course a recent change.

The 80,000 square kilometres of the Emirate of Abu Dhabi lie on the southeastern shores of the Arabian Gulf. Bounded by Qatar and Saudi Arabia in

*Dhows regularly race off the Abu Dhabi Corniche.*

*Abu Dhabi satellite image: A sophisticated network of roads and hundreds of high-rise towers now share the land.*

*Al Maqta'a Bridge links the island of Abu Dhabi with its hinterland.*

the west and southwest, by Oman in the south and east, and by the Emirates of Dubai and Sharjah in the northeast, it is made up mainly of arid gravel plains and sandy deserts, with large areas of *sabkha* (salt flats) along the coast. Offshore are several dozen islands, some large, such as Abu al-Abyadh, others little more than coral outcrops; while in the east, in the Al Ain area, the Emirate's border runs in the lee of the Hajar Mountain range. The whaleback of Jebel Hafit, south of Al Ain, is an outlying extension of the range.

The predominant feature is desert, but there are oases amid the sand, the best known of which are the large oasis of Al Ain in the east and the arc of small oases known as the Liwa in the south – the last secure source of water before the mountainous dunes of the Rub al-Khali.

Al Ain and the Liwa have traditionally been two of the four geographic pillars on which the Emirate stands, the third being the island of Abu Dhabi, capital both of the Emirate and of the UAE, and the fourth being the Western Islands, of which Sir Bani Yas and Dalma are today the most important. All of these have played a part in the history of the Emirate.

The emerging state of Abu Dhabi can be traced back to at least the late 16th century. In the latter years of that century, Gasparo Balbi, the court jew-

eller of the Serene Republic of Venice, toured the Gulf on his way to the East and published a book in 1590 in which he names some of the islands. Among them are Daas (Das), Zerecho (Zirku) and Delmephialmas (Dalma), but perhaps the most interesting of the names he reported was Sir Beni Ast, clearly the island known today as Sir Bani Yas. The reference is the first yet identified to the Bani Yas tribal confederation which, today led by Sheikh Zayed, is one of the four main tribal groupings making up the indigenous population of Abu Dhabi.

The Bani Yas themselves appear a few decades later, mentioned by name in an old history of Oman as having played a part in a war in the early 17th century that pitted the Omani Imams against a tribal alliance which included the Bani Yas and was led by one Nasser bin Qahtan al-Hilali. The Omani history refers to the Bani Yas making use of a fort in the al-Dhafra desert region, west of Abu Dhabi.

Coincidentally, work by the Abu Dhabi Islands Archaeological Survey in the al-Dhafra area, at Mantiqa al-Sirra, has now identified the remains of a long-lost fortress that appears to date from around the same period although, as yet, no link has been established.

By the late 17th century, the Al Nahyan family appears to have emerged as the undisputed leaders of the Bani Yas confederation, which was based in the Liwa Oasis on the edge of the Rub al-Khali. The Bani Yas shared the Liwa with the Manasir (Mansouris), another of the four tribal groupings that continue to play a major role in the Emirate today, and it was from the Liwa, or so the legend goes, that Sheikh Dhiyab bin Isa sent out a hunting party in 1761 that was to change the history of southern Arabia.

According to tribal tradition, the hunting party followed the track of a gazelle near the coast, and then across a narrow inlet at low tide. When the coastal mist lifted, they saw the gazelle drinking at a spring of brackish water. What happened to the gazelle is not related, but when the party returned to the Liwa to tell Sheikh Dhiyab of their discovery, he decreed that the island should be known as Abu Dhabi (the 'father' or possession of the gazelle). The truth may be somewhat more prosaic: archaeological evidence shows that the island was occupied much earlier, but there's little doubt that the modern settlement dates from around this time.

Recognising the importance of Abu Dhabi's water, a rare find along the Gulf coastline, Sheikh Dhiyab ordered a village to be established on the island. Although he chose to remain in Liwa, his son and successor, Sheikh Shakhbut bin Dhiyab, moved to the island in 1795 and Abu Dhabi has been the Emirate's capital ever since. He built a small fort around the spring. Much extended, that fort is today Qasr Al Hosn, long the home of the Ruling Family of Abu Dhabi and more recently the Government's Centre for Documentation and Research.

After Abu Dhabi and the Liwa, the third pillar of the growing Emirate was Al Ain. This was the traditional home of the powerful Dhawahir (Dhahiri) tribe, with whom Sheikh Shakhbut made an alliance early in the 19th century, building in 1818 a fort whose crumbling remains still survive. To complete the interlocking tribal alliances that made up the Emirate's population, the Bani Yas also established ties with the nomadic Awamir (Amiri) who roamed the desert to the south and west of Liwa.

The fourth geographic 'pillar', the Western Islands, owes its importance to the pearl beds in the surrounding waters which, archaeologists believe, may have been exploited for several thousand years until the trade finally faded away half a century ago.

The four tribes and the four geographical pillars, wherein most of the population lived, provided the foundations of the Emirate. The Al Ain Oasis, with its lush palm groves and ample supplies of subterranean water flowing through underground channels

*An attractive corner of Qasr Al Hosn.*

*Hundreds of tombs have been found on the top of Jebel Hafit near Al Ain. The best of the finds from here and other sites are on display at Al Ain Museum.*

(or *aflaj*; some as much as 3,000 years old), provided a simple agricultural base, supplemented by the smaller and poorer palms in Liwa and the sparse desert rangeland nearby.

The other main source of income was from the waters of the Gulf. The best pearl-oyster beds in the Gulf stretch across the great bay, extending eastwards from the Qatar Peninsula.

Traditionally, any local boat owner could search for pearls on the oyster beds, regardless of his place of origin. Once Sheikh Shakhbut had moved his headquarters to Abu Dhabi Island from the Liwa, the oyster beds all fell within Abu Dhabi's waters, giving the growing Emirate additional economic importance. While traders and pearl divers from other areas could continue to operate, they were permitted to do so only if they paid taxes to the Ruler.

Sheikh Shakhbut's own people also profited from the pearl harvest. A pattern of seasonal migration had long existed, allowing the best use to be made of the scanty resources both onshore and offshore. The Bani Yas was a confederation of sub-tribes (all of whom accepted the leadership of the Al Nahyan family), including the Suweidis, the Mazrouis, the Qamzis, the

*Dance has always played a central role in the traditions of the United Arab Emirates.*

When the British arrived in the area in 1820, they sought to persuade the Emirates along the coast to agree to an annual truce at sea during the pearling season and Abu Dhabi agreed to the plan with alacrity. The Treaty of Maritime Truce eventually became permanent – giving the area the name by which it was known until independence in 1971, the Trucial States.

From 1855 until 1909, during the reign of Sheikh Zayed bin Khalifa (Zayed the First), a grandson of Sheikh Shakhbut bin Dhiyab, Abu Dhabi rose to become a power throughout southeastern Arabia, with its influence stretching deep into inner Oman and the desert wastes of the Rub al-Khali, and up to what now comprises the northern Emirates.

Though the size of the Emirate declined in subsequent years, it retained much of its importance and strategic significance. When the oil wealth began to flow in the early 1960s, Abu Dhabi naturally took a prominent role in the formation of the United Arab Emirates under the present Ruler, Sheikh Zayed bin Sultan, grandson of Zayed the First.

*A dhow takes shape in the builder's yard near Batin village. Traditional tools are still used today.*

Hamilis, the Qubeisis and the Rumaithis.

Among some groups, the Hamilis and Qubeisis in particular, the winter months were spent harvesting dates in the Liwa or in the desert, while the men went offshore to the pearling grounds during the summer. Other groups, such as the Rumaithis and the Qamzis, could be found primarily along the coast and on the offshore islands, deriving their livelihood from fishing as well as pearls.

Control of the pearl grounds was an incentive for Abu Dhabi to ensure peace was maintained in the area, since any fighting would disrupt the pearl harvest.

*Typical Late Islamic pottery found at the Tawi Beduwa Shwaiba campsite south of Abu Dhabi.*

## Relics of an ancient past

If the origins of Abu Dhabi date back only 400 years or so, the history of the land and its people goes back much further. In recent years, archaeological excavations have shown that it played a prominent role in the development of civilisation in this corner of Arabia.

Fossil studies by palaeontologists from Britain's Natural History Museum and America's Yale University have shown that five or six million years ago, during the Late Miocene period, the land west of Abu Dhabi consisted of fertile plains and rivers, where early ancestors of elephants, horses and hippopotami lived. The rocks in which the fossils have been found, known as the Baynunah Formation, contain the most important array of fossils of land animals from the Late Miocene anywhere in the world.

It was not until much later, however, that people arrived in the Emirates. The first arrivals seem to have appeared during the Late Stone Age, 7,500 years ago. Isolated finds of flint implements in the desert can be dated back to around this period, as can flint-tool workshops found near Al Ain. Much of the most important evidence, however, has come from the offshore islands, thanks to work by the Government-backed Abu Dhabi Islands Archaeological Survey (Adias).

Under the patronage of UAE Chief of Staff, Lieutenant-General Sheikh Mohammed bin Zayed Al Nahyan, Adias has identified a major Late Stone Age site on the island of Marawah, where more than 200 fine flint tools have been recovered.

Results from excavations on the island of Dalma in the far west have been even more important. Here, Adias has discovered a permanent settlement, with houses up to eight metres in diameter and floors made of gypsum plaster. Finds of pottery imported from the early Ubaid civilisation in Mesopotamia show that the inhabitants of Dalma were already engaged in

*Excavated chambers of a traditional dwelling at Hili Archaeological Park in Al Ain.*

maritime trade, precursors of a tradition that has continued until today. Both the Marawah and Dalma sites are more than 7,000 years old, the oldest, at around 7,500 years, being that on Marawah.

There is further evidence of trading links from several thousand years or so later from the port-settlement of Umm al-Nar, adjacent to the island-city of Abu Dhabi, where the first archaeological excavations in the Emirates took place little more than 40 years ago.

The story of the discovery of the first ancient relics of Abu Dhabi's past is itself suitable for a detective novel. During the 1950s, a Danish team was excavating in Bahrain when the members were informed by a British amateur archaeologist working for Abu Dhabi Marine Areas – an oil company that is now part of the Abu Dhabi National Oil Company group – that there seemed to be burial mounds on Umm al-Nar.

When the Danes came to look, they found round tombs and a settlement dating back to the middle of the third millennium BC, from a culture that was hitherto unknown, and is now named the Umm al-Nar culture. The site also yielded finds that proved the people of Umm al-Nar were trading copper from the Hajar Mountains, near Al Ain, with Mesopotamia and the Indian subcontinent some 4,500 years ago.

Hearing of the Danish team's work, Sheikh Zayed, then Ruler's Representative in Al Ain, came to look at their finds. They should go to Al Ain as well, he told them, for on the foothills and the crest of nearby Jebel Hafit there were also piles of stones that might be worth examining.

Accepting Sheikh Zayed's invitation, the Danes travelled to Al Ain, to find literally hundreds of tombs on the top of Jebel Hafit, and on the tops of other mountains nearby, dating back to the early fourth-millennium BC. Those types of grave, now known from throughout the UAE's mountains, have been dubbed 'Hafit tombs.'

Such was the beginning of archaeology in Abu Dhabi – and since then, with the active encouragement of Sheikh Zayed, scarcely a year has passed without an excavation somewhere in the Emirate yielding new information about the area's past. In the early years, apart from Umm al-Nar, much of the work was concentrated in and around Al Ain.

An oasis for at least 5,000 years, its supplies of fresh water were as attractive to early inhabitants as they were in the recent past. Most interesting to the visitor is the complex of sites in the Hili area, which includes a number of settlements, a *falaj* dating back to around 1000 BC, and the now-famous Hili Tomb, a round stone structure with bas-relief carvings of

men and animals that has been carefully reconstructed. It now stands in the middle of one of Al Ain's lush public gardens, and, like many of the other local sites, can be freely visited.

More recently, the focus has turned to the coast and islands, where a whole range of important discoveries have been made by Adias. Among them are the Late Stone Age sites on Dalma and Marawah; Iron Age fireplaces on Rufayq island; pre-Islamic Christian monasteries on Marawah and Sir Bani Yas, the first evidence yet found of the presence of Christianity in the UAE before Islam; and the Late-Islamic fort at Mantiqa al-Sirra in the desert near Medinat Zayed.

The best of the finds from Umm al-Nar, Jebel Hafit, Hili and other sites in the Al Ain area are on display in the Al Ain Museum, which is housed next to the carefully modernised Eastern Fort. A major new national museum in Abu Dhabi is being planned.

## The people and their heritage

One popular part of the collection at the Al Ain Museum is an ethnographic display showing how the inhabitants of the Emirate lived in the days before oil – the Bedu tents, the simple farming implements, the camel saddles and old rifles, all are on display. So, too, are examples of local jewellery, and other items of

*Al Ain's Eastern Fort lies adjacent to the new museum.*

*An amazing feat of human strength – it requires no less than 70 and up to 100 men to pull the oars of a single racing boat through the water.*

everyday use, some of which can still be bought from antique shops in Al Ain and Abu Dhabi.

The display provides the visitor with a brief introduction to the heritage of the people of Abu Dhabi which, though lacking in written literature or imposing non-military architecture, is nevertheless of considerable interest. Deriving their livelihood both from the land and the sea, the people of Abu Dhabi had a culture before oil that reflected the influences of both – in their sports, in their poetry and in their way of life.

While the oral poetry, naturally, cannot be easily rendered into English, there is poetry enough in the physical aspects of the culture. The great days of the sailing dhows trading with China, India and East Africa, or of the pearling dhows that went out to harvest the Gulf's oysters, have now gone, but the tradition of sailing lives on.

Several times a year, there are races for sailing dhows just off the Abu Dhabi Corniche, and the sight of a couple of dozen or more triangular sails racing against the wind as similar sails have done for centuries has a poetry of its own. These races are sponsored by the government through the Emirates Heritage Club, which also supports another local maritime sport seen at the same time as the dhow races – rowing-boat racing. No coxed fours or eights these, each boat may have up to 100 oarsmen, chanting ageless rhythmic seamen's songs

*Oarsmen relax once they have crossed the finish line.*

*Few would deny harbouring a fascination with the falcon's exquisite appearance and precision in hunting.*

*Although camels are used today mainly as sporting or ceremonial animals, camel milk is still produced.*

as they pull their blades through the water.

The preservation of the country's traditional sports is accorded high priority by the government and Sheikh Zayed in particular. "A people that knows not its past has neither present nor future," Sheikh Zayed believes and, within that context, support has also been given to three land-based sports.

The most familiar to the visitor is horse-racing, both with the Thoroughbreds of Europe and North America, and with horses of Arab lineage, reintroduced to the area from the 1960s onwards. The horse has always been popular in Arabia, and Abu Dhabi has now emerged as a leader in the breeding of traditional Arabian horses. Races are held under the aegis of the UAE Equestrian Federation and the Emirates Arabian Horse Society.

Perhaps the most typical of local sports is falconry, still widely practised today, with saker or peregrine falcons bought from abroad or captured, then trained to answer to their master's voice.

Hunting the quarry, primarily birds such as the houbara bustard and the stone curlew, generally takes place abroad, since Abu Dhabi, and the rest of the UAE, now has strict conservation laws to curb local

hunting. Through Abu Dhabi's Environmental Research and Wildlife Development Agency (Erwda), however, experiments are being carried out into the captive breeding of the endangered houbara bustard which, it is hoped, will one day lead to the release of captive-bred birds to increase the wild population. Today, hunting is carried out from 4x4s but, until the advent of oil, falconers rode out on their camels, their falcons on their wrists.

Although no longer the preferred mode of transport, the camel remains an integral part of the lives of local people, who still keep camels for their milk, and the number of beasts in the Emirate continues to grow year by year, encouraged by Government subsidies for camel owners.

The main role of the camel in Abu Dhabi today, however, is not as a source of milk or as a means of transport, but as a sporting animal. Every winter, from October to April, camel races are held almost every weekend at tracks throughout the Emirates, culminating with the great annual races in April at Al Wathba, 40 kilometres east of Abu Dhabi, which attract top racers from across the Arabian Peninsula. With prizes totalling millions of dirhams at stake, it is not surprising that the top camels themselves are worth a considerable sum. Prices of five or six million dirhams are not unknown.

The races also provide an opportunity for the visitor to see local society at its most informal and democratic, with simple tribesmen from the desert rubbing shoulders with sheikhs in a common fascination with the sport.

The expatriate visitor is always welcome – as traditional Arab hospitality demands – but is always an outsider, a guest.

Arab hospitality remains the key to understanding the people of Abu Dhabi and their country. Forged in the harsh struggle of life before the coming of oil, the hospitality of the Bedu became a code of conduct. This tradition was so deep-rooted that a traveller coming across a desert encampment could always be sure of food and shelter from what little was available, even if on occasion his hosts were at the same time his tribal enemies.

A philosophy of sharing is part of the religion of Islam, which took hold in the area now known as the UAE during the lifetime of the Prophet Mohammed (PBUH). Today, it is a great strength to which the people of Abu Dhabi can hold fast amid the rapid changes that have swept away so much of their pre-

*A Bedouin woman, wearing a mask called a* burqa, *making a type of Arabic lace known as* telli.

vious way of life. It helps to provide, perhaps, a guarantee that however fast and far-reaching the changes, the essential nature of the culture and heritage of the desert people will remain.

*Two Abu Dhabi women in traditional dress embarking on an elaborate weaving project.*

*Chapter Four*

# Banking
# and commerce

TODAY, THE CITY OF ABU DHABI, AND THE EMIRATE OF which it is both the capital and the main population centre, has a thriving and diversified economy, with a modern infrastructure, social services, a world-class communications and transport system and an industrial base that ranges from petrochemicals and heavy industry to light manufacturing, agriculture and the services sector. Coupled with the possession of extensive international investment and reserves, it is well-equipped to grow steadily in the future.

Yet, little more than 40 years ago, the island city of Abu Dhabi itself was not much more than a poor coastal village while, inland, the way of life had hardly changed for centuries.

Traditionally, the people of Abu Dhabi survived in a subsistence economy. Fishing and – in the inland oases – agriculture provided the essentials of life for the settled people, while the nomadic tribes depended primarily on herding their livestock. In the east of the Emirate, in the mountains around Al Ain, ancient reserves of copper ore had been exploited from around 3000 BC, but this early local industry died out in the medieval period. Another industry, that of mining sulphur at Jebel Dhanna, in the west, had enjoyed a boom in the 17th and 18th centuries (when it was used in the making of gunpowder), but had also come to an end.

Offshore, another industry, that of collecting and selling the fine pearls found on the Gulf's oyster beds, had begun even earlier than the copper trade, and had thrived well into the 20th century. Unfortunately, the introduction of the Japanese cultured pearl, followed

*The modern, glass-clad skyscrapers of Abu Dhabi are the second generation of buildings on the island.*

by the world depression of the 1930s and the Second World War, dealt successive blows to the pearling industry and, by the early 1950s, it had virtually disappeared from the scene.

Just in time, another valuable resource was discovered – oil. Exploration began after the Second World War, and, after more than a decade of searching, the first commercially viable reserves were identified in the late 1950s.

In 1962, Abu Dhabi became an oil exporter for the first time. In the early years of Abu Dhabi's development, the growth sectors of the economy were based almost entirely on the oil industry. Employment, apart from a small but rapidly-growing civil service, was also heavily linked to the oil sector.

Throughout the years that followed, Abu Dhabi's economy has been underpinned by the oil industry, which has grown and matured despite the vicissitudes of the international oil market.

Revenues from oil and natural gas have enabled huge projects to be funded consecutively while the growth of the sector spawned a wide range of other industries. At the same time, the Government of Abu Dhabi, headed by Sheikh Zayed bin Sultan Al Nahyan, as Ruler, recognised that oil and gas were depletable resources that needed to be utilised with care and that it was unwise to permit a situation to continue where the health of the economy was dependent on one single source.

Through the Abu Dhabi Executive Council, chaired by Sheikh Khalifa bin Zayed Al Nahyan, the Crown Prince, various steps have been taken to lessen this dependence.

## A policy of diversification

In consequence, a carefully designed policy of diversification was set in motion. While the oil and gas industry still provides the bulk of government revenue, the economy as a whole has diversified to such an extent that, even in periods of weak oil prices, Abu Dhabi has continued to grow.

In 1968, when the first census was carried out, the Emirate had an estimated population of 46,500. By 2000, the population was estimated at 1.08 million, of whom 716,000 lived in the capital and its satellite townships on the mainland and a little more than 336,000 in and around Al Ain. Expatriates accounted for nearly 806,000 of the total and UAE citizens nearly 277,000.

The Emirate's workforce at the end of 2000 was around 533,000, of whom nearly 226,000 worked for

*The Emirates University in Al Ain provides higher education for nationals.*

*The eye-catching headquarters of Etisalat is one of Abu Dhabi's impressive landmarks.*

private companies and 165,000 for government, the remainder self-employed or working for individuals. The rate of unemployment was around 1.4 per cent.

The bulk of the Emirate's workforce is expatriate, largely from India and Pakistan, with large communities also from Iran, Afghanistan, Bangladesh, Sri Lanka and the Philippines. There are also significant communities from other Arab states such as Egypt and Syria, and from Europe and North America, in particular from Britain, France, the United States and Canada.

## The expansion of education among the country's citizens

With a rapidly rising number of UAE citizens, the government, supported by the private sector, has launched a programme of 'Emiratisation,' which is leading to a growing number of citizens, both men and women, entering the workforce. Besides government ministries and departments, this process is particularly visible in the oil and gas sector and in the finance industry. Overall, citizens of the country account for a quarter of the UAE's total population, which was estimated at around 3.2 million in mid-2001.

Key sectors of employment are the civil service, including both federal ministries and departments of the local government; the services sector, including banking, finance and the hospitality industry; the industrial sector, covering both the oil and gas industry and other light industries, transport and communications and agriculture.

## Gross domestic product

The oil and gas industry in Abu Dhabi, operating primarily through the framework of the state-owned Abu Dhabi National Oil Company (Adnoc) is controlled by guidelines laid down by the Emirate's Supreme Petroleum Council, chaired by Crown Prince Sheikh Khalifa bin Zayed, and is separately profiled in Chapter 5.

While the oil and gas sector is government-controlled, in other areas of the economy the rules of the free market apply, with the free transfer of capital and profits and (an important factor for expatriate residents) free transfer of earnings, coupled with a firm adherence to a policy of no taxation on personal or corporate incomes.

The GDP of Abu Dhabi can be sharply affected by fluctuations in oil prices. In 1997, for example, it stood at around Dh103 billion, falling to Dh89.2 billion in 1998 and rising to Dh107.7 billion in 1999. In

2000, it rose to Dh145.4 billion, falling again in 2001 because of a drop in oil prices.

Increasingly, however, the impact of changes in oil prices is being offset by the steadily rising contribution from the non-oil sector, which provided 49.5 per cent of the Emirate's GDP in 2000, mainly from manufacturing (including petrochemicals), followed by government services, housing and construction. Total non-oil exports through Abu Dhabi in 2000 amounted to Dh982 million.

In 2000, per-capita income for the Emirate's 1.08 million inhabitants was around Dh132,000, or nearly US$36,000 – one of the highest in the world.

## The financial sector

Thanks partly to oil and gas revenues, and partly to the demand for financial services arising out of the industry, Abu Dhabi now has an extensive and sophisticated financial sector. The capital city is the headquarters of the Arab Monetary Fund, the Arab world's equivalent of the International Monetary Fund, while it also has the head office of another pan-Arab financial institution, the Arab Bank of Investment and Foreign Trade, which is partly owned by the Abu Dhabi Government.

Based in Abu Dhabi, the UAE Central Bank supervises the local institutions and regulates the activities of all foreign banks in the Emirates, as well as currency exchange houses and financial advisers. Formed in 1981, the Central Bank owes its origins to the former UAE Currency Board, established after the creation of the federation to act as an issuer of currency and government lender, but was equipped with greater authority and powers to regulate the financial community.

Moving cautiously over the years, the Central Bank has been an effective force for stability and has enabled the economy to weather a number of crises. Some arose from the collapse of local banks, often as a result of poor lending policies. Depositors, however, have never been allowed to suffer, and the Central Bank has discreetly used its powers to encourage the weaker local banks to merge, or to agree to being taken over.

With more than Dh52.9 billion in assets in mid-2001, the Central Bank has the strength to play a key role in the economy of the UAE, and has successfully maintained a formal link between the dirham and the dollar, the currency in which crude oil prices are designated, despite the fluctuations of international currency markets.

The first bank in Abu Dhabi, a branch of the

*The traditional minaret of a mosque contrasts strongly with the modern plate glass of an office building.*

*More than 700,000 people live in the city of Abu Dhabi and its satellite townships on the mainland.*

British Bank of the Middle East, now HSBC, was opened only in 1959. The banking sector now includes a number of important institutions, both local and international. There are five Abu Dhabi-based local banks, of which the National Bank of Abu Dhabi is the largest. Among Arab banks, it was 15th overall in its total assets: around US$8.8 billion at the end of 2001, a year in which it recorded its highest-ever net profits, some US$165 million.

Moving up fast in the regional rankings are the Abu Dhabi Commercial Bank, formed from a merger of three smaller banks in the mid-1980s, with total assets at the end of 2001 of US$7.25 billion and net profits of US$166 million, and Union National Bank, whose total assets at the end of 2001 were around US$3.6 billion.

The Abu Dhabi Islamic Bank, said to be the largest Islamic financial institution in the world, with paid up capital of one billion dirhams (US$270 million), began full operations in early 1999. Operating in accordance with Sharia law, it has introduced innovative new financial instruments to the local market, and had total assets of US$1.66 billion at the end of 2001.

The fifth bank, First Gulf Bank, although the smallest, is growing quickly, recording its highest-ever profit in 2001, with total assets in that year rising by 42 per cent to US$930 million.

Banks from the other Emirates also have branches in Abu Dhabi, as do many major global banks, all competing for a share of the lucrative market for institutional business, trade finance and personal banking. Overall, there are 20 locally incorporated banks in the Emirates and 29 foreign banks, including a restricted-licence bank and two investment banks, most of which have offices in Abu Dhabi.

Besides the banking sector, Abu Dhabi has a number of other financial institutions. Of particular importance are the currency exchange houses, of which 49 have offices in the city, including 20 head offices. Some are little more than money changers in the souk, but others are major financial institutions in their own right, handling hundreds of millions of dollars a year in currency exchange, transfers and drafts. Their services are particularly valued by Abu Dhabi's expatriate labour force, many of whom come

*Abu Dhabi has a vibrant commercial sector with 34,000 companies belonging to its Chamber of Commerce.*

from rural areas in countries such as India, Pakistan and the Philippines where the indigenous banking system is poorly developed.

These currency exchanges, like the banks, are subject to regulation by the Central Bank to ensure that they are not used for illegal money transfers. There is also a plethora of companies offering financial advice, as well as firms of share brokers handling the buying and selling of stocks and shares in local companies.

The local stock exchange, the Abu Dhabi Securities Market, was formally established in 1999 to regularise trading in securities and offers opportunities for trading in a number of listed local stocks, including key firms such as the locally-incorporated banks, telecommunications giant Etisalat and industrial enterprises such as Abu Dhabi Shipbuilding. The market is linked to another trading floor in Dubai, and together the two have opened up greater opportunities for UAE citizens and companies to invest in local firms.

Once the door is opened to foreign investors, which will eventually take place because of World Trade Organisation rules, a steady flow of inward investment is likely to stimulate market growth.

A much less visible part of the financial community is the Abu Dhabi Investment Authority (Adia), established before the creation of the UAE to act as fund manager for Abu Dhabi's surplus oil revenues. Adia has become one of the world's major investment institutions and, although it never gives any indication of the total funds under its management, a cautious estimate suggests that these are well in excess of US$150 billion. Its basic function is to provide a guarantee for Abu Dhabi's future, and it has shown considerable success in performing that task. In some years, its income from investments, largely overseas, is believed to exceed Abu Dhabi's entire oil revenues.

## A vibrant commercial sector

Abu Dhabi's vibrant commercial sector is supervised by the government-supported Abu Dhabi Chamber of Commerce and Industry, which had nearly 34,000 member companies at the end of 2000. Routine services for members include an extensive data bank

*The Emirate is served by an excellent road network, with many attractive green areas.*

and an arbitration service, of particular value for problems relating to agency agreements with foreign firms, as well as conference facilities and a dedicated e-mail service.

Through its international relations section, the chamber also hosts numerous overseas trade missions every year, helping to introduce local business people to their foreign counterparts and, where necessary, providing advice on the conclusion of partnership or agency agreements.

According to the chamber's president, one key objective during the period from 2002 to 2006 is to project Abu Dhabi at a global level as an ideal investment-and-business centre for the Arabian Gulf region.

One important part of this objective is the promotion of Abu Dhabi as a centre for international exhibitions and conferences, a process with which the chamber has long been associated. Until the late 1990s, the chamber's own exhibitions department was responsible for certain events, while the Military Committee for Defence Exhibitions, Codex, was responsible for military shows, organising in alternate years the International Defence Exhibition (Idex) and the Triple Defence Exhibition (Tridex), each having a slightly different emphasis.

Now, however, the chamber and the military have joined together to establish the government-owned General Exhibitions Corporation (GEC), which has taken over responsibility for all exhibitions on a purpose-built site on the outskirts of the city, which is already well provided with exhibition halls, as well as an external display arena. A World Trade Centre, including office and residential accommodation, a hotel and other facilities should be in operation by 2004 or 2005. The first phase, with 100,000 square metres of space, is expected to cost around US$109 million.

The Idex/Tridex exhibitions, which began in 1993, have already established Abu Dhabi as the most important centre for defence exhibitions outside Western Europe, and attract the world's major defence manufacturers as exhibitors as well as senior government and military personnel from around the world. So important has the series become that Abu Dhabi has frequently been chosen by arms manufacturers to launch their new products.

A key to the success of Idex and Tridex has been the military-expenditure plans not only of the UAE, but also for the whole of the Middle East and West Asian regions, which are now the world's biggest market for new defence equipment.

*The Etisalat tower, with its hallmark sphere, is reflected in the glass of a neighbouring building.*

*Gulf Air has a major presence in Abu Dhabi and is the national carrier of Abu Dhabi, Bharain and Oman.*

Closely associated with the UAE's defence acquisition programme is the innovative UAE Offsets Programme, under which any manufacturer winning a defence contract worth more than US$10 million from the Emirates must in return invest an amount equivalent to 60 per cent of the total value of the contract in joint ventures in the UAE. Huge sums are involved. Two contracts alone – with GIAT of France for battle tanks, and with McDonnell Douglas of the United States for F-16 fighter aircraft – involve offset obligations of more than one-billion dollars.

Not surprisingly, implementation of the programme took some time to get under way but, by the end of 2001, 21 joint ventures, ranging from shipbuilding, fish farming and financial services to agriculture, medical-waste management and training and business centres were in operation. Of these, several have operations not just in Abu Dhabi, but elsewhere in the UAE and also overseas. One such is the Oasis International Leasing Company, a joint venture with major manufacturer British Aerospace as a partner, which is the region's only major leasing firm.

Initial projects, worth many hundreds of millions of dollars, included aircraft-lease deals with Gulf Air and planning for a similar arrangement with the shipping subsidiaries of Adnoc. Another is the International Fish Farming Company, Asmak, with operations or interests in Fujairah, Ra's al-Khaimah, Oman, Kuwait and Greece.

One result of the Offsets Programme has been the creation of wealth for national citizens. More than 100,000 UAE citizens are shareholders in four of the larger projects that have offered shares to the public, which between them have a total capital of more than Dh 2.5 billion.

The Offsets Programme, supervised by Chief of Staff Lt General Sheikh Mohammed bin Zayed Al Nahyan, has been of particular value in its insistence that there should be a major emphasis on the transfer of skills and technology. It has now also matured into an industrial development agency and venture-capital organisation, and acts as a think-tank for the government on a variety of strategic initiatives in the oil and gas and other sectors.

The determination of the government to encourage the private sector, and to provide opportunities for local investment to absorb surplus liquidity, can also be seen in the developing programme of privatisation of utilities and other services.

Under the terms of this programme, Abu Dhabi's water and electricity sector was completely reorganised in the late 1990s, with the objective of driving down whole sector costs and improving operational and customer service performance. It now operates through the Abu Dhabi Water and Electricity Authority (Adwea), under which six separate power-generation and desalination companies have been established to run the power plants.

Of these, the largest is the Taweela complex, now being expanded to a production capacity of

*Gulf Aircraft Maintenance Company (Gamco) is an important aviation maintenance centre.*

84.76-million gallons of desalinated water a day and an installed electricity capacity of 1,431 megawatts.

Work got under way in late 2001 on another huge plant near Shuweihat, in the Western Region, which, when completed at a cost of around US$1.6 billion, will produce a further 1,000 million gallons a day and another 1,500 megawatts. The plant is being developed as a joint venture between Adwea and foreign utility firms. Other major plants are at Mirfa and Umm al-Nar. Separate companies have been established to handle transmission and distribution to the Emirate's 300,000 industrial and domestic customers.

In the Emirate of Abu Dhabi as a whole, demand for electricity is expected to rise by more than 10 per cent a year until 2004, with a more than eight per cent growth a year in demand for water, and the investment in this sector now represents one of the fastest growing areas of the local economy. Much is coming from international utility companies, with firms from the United States, Britain, France and Belgium all involved.

## Modern infrastructure

Since the UAE was founded in 1971, substantial investment has been made in the very best in modern communications. A fine road network connects the capital with Dubai and the other northern Emirates, with inland Al Ain, and with the oil industry town of Ruwais in the west.

The highway to Ruwais continues on through the Ghuweifat border post into Saudi Arabia. Other roads run deep into the desert, to the major oilfields and on to the agricultural centre of the Liwa Oasis on the edge of the Rub al-Khali. In all, the Emirate has more than 1,500 kilometres of highways, excluding internal roads in the major population centres.

The construction of a railway has also been suggested, although no decision is likely to be taken unless such a network can be linked to the rest of the Arabian Peninsula.

Also facilitating internal and external communications is the state-of-the-art telecommunications network provided by state-owned Etisalat, which at the end of 2001 had more than 260,000 fixed lines and 621,000 mobile lines in Abu Dhabi as well as nearly 68,000 Internet dial-up subscribers. Direct dialling is available to more than 150 countries, while Etisalat, through the locally-based regional satellite firm Thuraya, is emerging as the Middle East's leader in the telecommunications industry.

Transport connections with the rest of the world are provided through excellent air and sea links. Abu Dhabi International Airport, 40 kilometres outside the city, handles more than 3,500,000 passengers and 65,000 aircraft movements a year and is served by 40 airlines, with scheduled flights to nearly 90 destinations. A Dh2.2 billion expansion programme to meet passenger and airline industry demand for a decade or so to come should be completed by 2005.

***The bulk of Abu Dhabi's shipping industry is focused on the growing international port of Mina Zayed.***

This will include a second runway and expanded passenger and freight facilities, including a new terminal, along with a five-star hotel and leisure centre. The subsidiary airport at Al Ain, a little more than 100 kilometres to the east, is also being expanded.

A popular attraction at Abu Dhabi Airport is its duty-free complex, winner of numerous international awards, whose shops handle around US$80 million of business every year.

Located on a site adjacent to the airport, Gulf Aircraft Maintenance Company (Gamco), provides all routine maintenance for the fleet of regional carrier Gulf Air, itself partly owned by Abu Dhabi. Gamco, with special expertise in Airbus aircraft and the Lockheed Tristar, has attracted a growing number of customers from around the world, often beating tough competition. One such core customer is Britain's Royal Air Force, which has chosen Gamco to undertake all maintenance for its Tristar transport fleet.

The airport is also the base of Abu Dhabi Aviation, the largest commercial-helicopter operator in the Middle East, with 33 aircraft. It also has two fixed-wing aircraft and employs some 60 pilots and 100 maintenance personnel. Much of its work is undertaken for the local oil and construction industries, although the firm also operates in Oman, Yemen,

Saudi Arabia, Kuwait and elsewhere in the region.

While the oil and gas industry operates its own ports and terminals, the bulk of Abu Dhabi's shipping industry is focused on Mina (Port) Zayed, on the island of Abu Dhabi itself.

Although still a relatively small player in the country's shipping industry as a whole, handling less than 10 per cent of total container throughput, Mina Zayed has ample space for more business and is growing steadily in line with other sectors of the local economy. Nearly four million tons of general cargo and containers and more than 25,000 vehicles were discharged at the port in the year 2000.

The adjacent free zone with its many warehouses has grown in recent years to become a major industrial storage and bulk wholesale zone. To complement this, a plan for the development of the ancillary fishing and local trade market and quay area, which will promote Mina Zayed as a trading complex as well as enhance its ability to handle the growing maritime links with other Gulf countries, was announced in early 2002.

The rapidly growing local economy and population has stimulated a growth in imports during the last three decades while, aside from oil and gas products, the export sector has also grown substantially.

The development of the manufacturing sector has produced goods surplus to local requirements, with new markets being actively developed elsewhere in the region. Also of significance is the transit and re-export trade, much of which is carried by road from Mina Zayed to destinations elsewhere in the Arabian Peninsula.

This removes the need for shipping to venture further up the Arabian Gulf, where higher shipping insurance rates apply.

Excluding the UAE's fellow member states in the Arab Gulf Co-operation Council (AGCC), Abu Dhabi's major trade partner is Japan, which imports more than a quarter of its entire energy needs from the UAE, primarily from Abu Dhabi. Other major export markets include the United States, Britain, China, India, South Korea, the other AGCC countries and Iran.

Total imports in 2000 exceeded US$5.6 billion, with non-oil exports and re-exports worth slightly more than US$580 million. Exports of oil and gas, as well as of petroleum products and other by-products of the oil industry, are sufficient to ensure a healthy positive trade balance, although their value is, inevitably, affected by fluctuations in the world oil market.

*A second satellite terminal at Abu Dhabi International Airport should be completed in 2005.*

## Chapter Five

# The oil and gas sector

THE UNITED ARAB EMIRATES, OF WHICH ABU DHABI IS a part, is one of the fastest growing states in the world. Half a century ago, life in the Emirates was little changed from what it had been hundreds of years earlier. As recently as the early 1970s, just after the UAE itself was formed, Abu Dhabi, today a thriving modern metropolis, was still a small town. The pace of growth has been dramatic.

While much of the credit belongs to the country's Rulers, led by President His Highness Sheikh Zayed bin Sultan Al Nahyan, little could have been achieved without the revenues from oil and gas production, which have underpinned the economy and have provided the fuel for growth. In the words of Sheikh Zayed: "Oil is useless if it is not exploited for the welfare of the citizen," and in the years since 1966, when he became Ruler of Abu Dhabi, the country's oil wealth has indeed been used to provide the people of the Emirates with all the facilities of a modern welfare state.

Today, the UAE is one of the world's top oil producers, with its proven recoverable reserves of around 98 billion barrels being the third largest in the world. With around 6.2 trillion cubic metres of gas reserves as well (the fourth largest in the world), the country is well equipped to continue production of both oil and gas in substantial quantities for more than a century. In excess of 90 per cent of those oil reserves are in the Emirate of Abu Dhabi, whose people are among the richest on earth in terms of per capita income.

It is less than 45 years since the first commercially viable oil discovery was made in Abu Dhabi, and production did not begin until the early 1960s.

*At the spudding-in ceremony at Ra's Sadr, Abu Dhabi's first oil well, in 1950.*

*Jack-up rigs stacked in Abu Dhabi's Mina Zayed.*

Nevertheless, the history of the Emirate's oil industry can be traced back more than 60 years.

Oil production began in Iraq and Iran prior to the First World War but, at the time, little attention was paid to the southern Gulf. In the early 1930s, however, the discovery of oil further north in the Arabian Peninsula – in Bahrain and Saudi Arabia – sparked the interest of the major western oil companies in the little known Emirates of the lower Gulf, the largest of which was Abu Dhabi.

Front runner in the field was the consortium of for-eign oil companies forming the Iraq Petroleum Company (IPC). They included British Petroleum (BP), Shell and the companies now known as TotalFinaElf and ExxonMobil, as well as the family interests of famed Armenian entrepreneur Calouste Gulbenkian, the original 'Mr Five Per Cent'. In the mid-1930s, IPC sought and obtained permission to venture into the Emirates.

The first step was to send teams of surveyors to see whether there were any surface indications of oil or any interesting geological structures. Visiting the offshore islands was easy: the first known landing of a motor vehicle on Abu Dhabi's western island of Sir Bani Yas dates back to this time, when an oil company survey party put a truck ashore to help them move around.

Venturing inland, however, was much more difficult. At the time, little was known about the desert areas of Abu Dhabi except by local inhabitants. Indeed, it was not until the late 1940s that the first European explorer, Sir Wilfred Thesiger, set sight on the Liwa Oasis after one of his epic crossings of the Empty Quarter. There was also no guarantee that the Bedu of the desert would welcome the visitors.

The ruler of Abu Dhabi, Sheikh Shakhbut bin Sultan Al Nahyan, elder brother and predecessor of His Highness Sheikh Zayed, welcomed the wish of the oil companies to start exploring, although naturally he was also concerned that they should help in finding new supplies of fresh water for the people. To show his own backing for their enterprise, he assigned the young Sheikh Zayed to accompany them.

Initial signs were promising and, on January 11, 1939, after several years of negotiations, Sheikh Shakhbut signed an exploration concession with an IPC subsidiary, Petroleum Concessions Limited (PCL), which covered the whole of the territory of Abu Dhabi for a period of 75 years. PCL established its own subsidiary, Petroleum Concessions (Trucial Coast), to operate this concession and others it won elsewhere in the Emirates. Later renamed Petroleum Development (Trucial Coast) and then finally the Abu Dhabi Petroleum Company, it continued to operate onshore until 1979, when it handed over the task to a new joint-venture company.

Plans to examine the new concession area were delayed by the Second World War, and it was not until the later 1940s that exploration began in earnest. Using sturdy vehicles and engaging Bedu as guides, the geologists spread out across the land to choose the site for their first well.

## Onshore fields

The site chosen was at Ra's Sadr, on the coast some 35 kilometres northeast of Abu Dhabi, where the spudding-in of the UAE's first oil well took place in 1950. The operation was not without incident and drama. All the equipment had to be brought in by barge to Ra's Ghanadha, a few kilometres further east, then brought overland to the drilling site. At one point, dissatisfied with their conditions of employment, the locally-hired Abu Dhabian workforce

*Jack-up rigs being prepared for the exploration of Abu Dhabi's offshore fields.*

downed tools and, in the last recorded use of British 'gunboat diplomacy' in the Gulf, a force of Royal Marines was landed to bring the dispute to an end.

Former IPC official Ronald Codrai (author of several books published by Motivate Publishing) recalled years later that there was an element of farce to the affair. The boats used by the Royal Marines grounded in the shallow waters and they were obliged to seek help from local fishermen to get to Ra's Sadr. Fortunately, wiser counsels prevailed, and another brother of Sheikh Shakhbut, Sheikh Hazza, persuaded the oil company to improve its terms, and encouraged its employees to go back to work.

At the time it was drilled, the Ra's Sadr-1 well, at more than 13,000 feet, was the deepest ever drilled in the Middle East – early proof that the local oil industry was to be at the forefront of petroleum technology. It was, though, a dry hole, as was a second well drilled at Shuweihat, near Jebel Dhanna. A third, at Murban, west of Abu Dhabi and in the heart of the desert, found promising traces of hydrocarbons. Further drilling ensued and, in 1960, a third well on the Murban structure proved the commercial

**Seabed surveys made by Jacques Cousteau were vital.**

viability of what was to become known as the Bab field, Abu Dhabi's first onshore oil discovery.

## Offshore drilling

The search for oil had also begun offshore. In 1951, in what was to prove a landmark decision in international law, Sheikh Shakhbut decided to award a separate concession to cover Abu Dhabi's territorial waters outside the three-mile limit. The first concessionaire gave up in 1953 after a limited exploration effort, a decision they doubtless later came to regret. A year later, a new concession was awarded to Abu Dhabi Marine Areas (Adma), established by British Petroleum and Total (now TotalFinaElf), but later also to have a small Japanese shareholding.

Initial surveys of the seabed promptly began, led by the world-famous French underwater explorer, Commander Jacques-Yves Cousteau. Operating from his research ship *Calypso*, Cousteau and his team spent a total of 67 days studying the seabed and, on the basis of his findings, Adma decided to drill a first well at a location known as Umm Shaif.

In 1996, on the occasion of the UAE's Silver Jubilee, and in recognition of his valuable contribu-

**Much of Abu Dhabi's oil wealth comes from offshore, where giant platforms such as this TotalFinaElf structure are operated with foreign partners.**

tion to the country's development, Commander Cousteau was decorated by President Sheikh Zayed.

Once again, Abu Dhabi's infant oil industry was at the cutting edge of new technology. A special drilling barge, *Adma Enterprise*, was constructed in Europe and towed out to the Gulf where, operating from a base on Das Island, it began work in January 1958. Less than three months later, there was success. The Umm Shaif-1 well struck oil in commercial quantities. The oil era had begun.

Developing the newly-discovered fields took time, with the companies and their employees battling onshore against the harsh desert terrain and, offshore, working against the limits of known technology under the waters of the Gulf.

One of the first tasks was to choose suitable sites for terminals from which the oil could be exported. Onshore, a site was selected at Jebel Dhanna, a small hill in the far west from where oil could flow by gravity into the oil tankers. The painstaking job of laying the pipeline across the desert began.

Offshore, Das Island, once only a home for thousands of nesting sea birds, turtles and the occasional fisherman, was selected. At both locations, new facilities had to be built to treat the oil, as well as house the workforce, and this took some time to complete. Adma won the race to build its facilities and the first cargo of oil from Umm Shaif and Abu Dhabi left from Das on 4 July, 1962. The first cargo of crude from the Bab field followed in December 1963.

This was only the start. Onshore, field after field was discovered as exploration continued. The giant Bu Hasa field and the smaller Asab, Sahil and Shah fields followed, all subsequently being brought into production. During the past few years, yet more have followed, at Rumaitha, Shanayel and Dabb'iya, these now being developed to produce around 110,000 barrels a day by mid-2005.

Offshore, Adma followed up its success at Umm Shaif by discovering another giant field, Zakum, as well as several smaller fields. The planned relinquishment of part of the concession area later saw several other companies either develop Adma finds, or make their own discoveries. These include Abu al-Bukhoosh, Mubarraz, Satah, Umm al-Dalkh and several smaller fields (all now in production), while a number of other finds, such as Nasr and Umm Lulu, have been proven and kept in reserve for the future.

As the industry grew and production expanded, so the political scene in Abu Dhabi changed. In August 1966, Sheikh Zayed succeeded his brother Sheikh Shakhbut as Ruler of Abu Dhabi, becoming President of the new Federation of the United Arab Emirates in 1971.

*Adma-Opco has a super-complex at Umm Shaif in Abu Dhabi waters.*

*Continued exploration and development of oil wells ensures that maximum production capacity is achieved.*

## Joint ventures

During the next few years, the world's major oil-producing countries – among them the UAE – gradually changed their relationship with the international oil companies, extending their own control over the key, but depletable, resource.

In Abu Dhabi, this was marked first by the establishment in 1971 of the Abu Dhabi National Oil Company (Adnoc) to represent government oil interests and to act as owner of an associated resource whose importance was slowly becoming recognised – that of natural gas.

The signing of participation agreements with the shareholders in ADPC and Adma followed, with the Government's percentage in the oil concessions rising in two stages to 60 per cent by the late 1970s. New joint venture operating companies were formed, ADPC being replaced by the Abu Dhabi Company for Onshore Oil Operations (Adco) and Adma by the Abu Dhabi Marine Operating Company (Adma-Opco), in which the foreign shareholders retained a 40-per-cent stake.

Another joint venture operating firm, the Zakum Development Company (Zadco), was also set up to operate the reservoirs of the Upper Zakum field, and was later also given responsibility for the Umm al-Dalkh and Satah fields. Adnoc originally held 88 per cent of the shares, and the Japan Oil Development Company (Jodco) the remaining 12 per cent, although this was revised in 1994 to 51 per cent Adnoc and 49 per cent Jodco.

In each case, however, the foreign shareholders retained a share in the oil concessions and the reserves themselves. The approach was unique in the major oil-producing states of the Arabian Gulf, and was adopted by Adnoc and the Government of Abu Dhabi partly to ensure continued access to the very latest in oil industry technological expertise.

Through the years, the approach has paid off: Abu Dhabi is now a world leader in techniques such as horizontal drilling and enhanced oil recovery. A foreign presence is also evident in some of the smaller fields, such as Abu al-Bukhoosh (operated by the French oil company, TotalFinaElf), and Mubarraz, Umm al-Anbar and Neewat al-Ghalan (operated by the Abu Dhabi Oil Company (Japan), where Adnoc has no shareholding at all. Production levels for these companies, as for the Adnoc Group, are set by the Abu Dhabi Supreme Petroleum Council (SPC), whose chairman is Abu Dhabi's Crown Prince, Sheikh Khalifa bin Zayed.

Production in late 2002 was around 1.9 million barrels per day (bpd), in accordance with the quota

59

*Modern methods of seismic surveying unlock the secrets of the desert.*

assigned to the UAE by the Organisation of Petroleum Exporting Countries (Opec), and can vary both upwards and downwards. Installed sustainable production capacity, however, is much higher, and is now more than 2.6 million bpd.

One proud claim of Abu Dhabi's oil industry is that its extensive and continuing exploration programme during the past 40 years has generally meant that new discoveries match, or even exceed, the volume of oil actually produced each year. There can be few better guarantees of the Emirate's long-term prosperity.

## Natural gas

Together with the oil discoveries have come finds of natural gas, of which some, but by no means all, are associated with oil-bearing reservoirs. At the time that the early oil concession agreements were signed, there was little recognition of the potential importance of natural gas, which was not included. As a result, the gas reserves, whether associated or non-associated, belong in their entirety to the Government of Abu Dhabi.

Until the mid-1970s, virtually all the associated gas from the oilfields was flared off, creating the eerie night landscape of flames once so familiar to visitors arriving in Abu Dhabi by air. At the same time, it wasted a valuable natural resource and polluted the atmosphere.

A programme to end waste was set up in the late 1970s, with the decision by Adnoc – in association with foreign partners, including BP, Shell, TotalFinaElf and Japanese interests – to establish two companies to harness and utilise the associated gas supplies. While some gas is reinjected into the oil reservoirs, to maintain pressure and enhance oil recovery, much is now used for local industry and for export.

Onshore, Abu Dhabi Gas Industries Limited (Gasco) was established to handle gas from the Adco fields, while offshore the Abu Dhabi Gas Liquefaction Company (Adgas), was created. Gasco and Adco produce their gas and oil from fields that, for the most part, lie deep in the desert. From there, after initial treatment, it is transferred by a network of pipelines, run by Gasco, to a central point at Habshan, a little north of the growing desert township of Bida Zayed.

Here, more gas from non-associated fields and reservoirs joins and further treatment takes place. It is then transferred along more pipelines. One line goes northeast to Abu Dhabi, where the gas is used for power at the Umm al-Nar industrial complex and power plant, and further on to the world's largest water desalination and power generation plant at Taweela, on the coast northeast of Abu Dhabi. A spur line also runs across the desert to the inland oasis city of Al Ain.

Another extension line runs from Taweela northeast to Dubai's Jebel Ali industrial zone, helping to provide the power upon which Dubai's industries depend.

The second gas line from Habshan runs northwest to the Ruwais industrial zone, just east of Adco's oil-export terminal at Jebel Dhanna. Here, the clean natural gas liquids (NGLs) are split by a fractionation process into propane, butane and pentane. The bulk of this is then exported, although increasingly it is being put to good use in the local market as, for example, feedstock for petrochemicals.

The Ruwais zone is the centre of the Adnoc group's downstream projects. Here are found, for example, the UAE's largest refinery and a 280,000-bpd condensate splitter (both operated by Takreer, an Adnoc subsidiary), a sulphur plant, a hydrocracker unit and, largest of all, Borouge, a massive petrochemicals project that came into operation in late 2001.

A joint venture between Adnoc and industry-leader Borealis, in which the Government of Abu Dhabi has a stake through its International Petroleum Investment Company (Ipic), the Borouge plant and associated facilities cost nearly one billion US dollars to build, and is one of the largest polyethylene production facilities in the Middle East. Virtually all of its output is sold overseas.

With the increasing demand for gas both as feedstock for plants in the Ruwais zone and as fuel for industries and other consumers elsewhere in the UAE, a new gas line is being built from the offshore Umm Shaif oilfield to the Gasco facilities at Habshan.

Offshore, Adgas and Adma-Opco share facilities on Das Island. Here gas from the offshore oilfields is collected and treated, producing liquefied natural gas (LNG) and liquefied petroleum gas (LPG). Initially, all the LNG was exported to Japan, under a long-term contract with the Tokyo Electric Power Company (Tepco).

However, a doubling of Adgas capacity in the mid-1990s, to 5.4 million tonnes a year, coupled with changing patterns of energy consumption in Japan, made it necessary for Adgas to seek additional markets. Against tough competition, the company now sells to other countries in East Asia and Europe, and further expansion of the Das plant to 6.4 million tonnes a year is being planned.

As the range of products from the Adnoc Group has grown, so it has been obliged to diversify. From the mid-1970s, for example, its majority shareholding in the oil concessions gave Adnoc its own crude oil to market. The rapid expansion of the local economy and the building and subsequent expansion of refineries first at Umm al-Nar and then Ruwais provided a captive and growing local market for refined fuels.

Operated by Adnoc subsidiary Takreer, the refineries now have a capacity to process 500,000 bpd of oil and condensate. Through its wholly-owned subsidiary, the Abu Dhabi National Oil Company for Distribution (Adnoc-Fod), which operates in the northern Emirates as well as in Abu Dhabi, fuel for household use, cars, aircraft and shipping is now supplied by Adnoc.

Despite the growth in this home-based demand,

*Continued success in Abu Dhabi's extensive oil-exploration programme during the past 40 years has guaranteed the Emirate's long-term prosperity.*

Adnoc has millions of barrels of crude oil a year available for export, primarily on long-term contracts. Rather than rely entirely on chartering tankers, Adnoc created its own shipping firm, the Abu Dhabi National Tanker Company (Adnatco), whose fleet of seven tankers carries Adnoc oil to markets around the world.

The establishment of the gas industry required yet more ships. The Natural Gas Shipping Company (NGSCO) is responsible for the shipment of LNG from the Adgas facility on Das Island, and now operates eight of the largest gas carriers in the world.

## Industry expansion

The Adnoc Group also comprises a number of other firms, some of which have grown to become industry leaders. These include the Abu Dhabi Petroleum Ports Operating Company (Adppoc), which handles the export terminals; Abu Dhabi Drilling and Chemical Products Company (Addcap), manufacturing chemicals for the industry; National Marine Services; the National Drilling Company, which with

22 rigs is one of the largest drilling firms in the Middle East, and Ruwais Fertiliser Industries (Fertil), which exports its products around the world.

A particular success has been the National Petroleum Construction Company (NPCC), which not only builds offshore jackets and platforms for installation in Abu Dhabi's oilfields, but has also won contracts to build massive structures for other countries, including India and Iran.

From its initial base as a crude oil producer, the Abu Dhabi oil industry has expanded and diversified so that the production of oil itself, though key to the whole process, now represents the core of an industrial and transportation sector that includes gas production, petrochemicals, heavy engineering, shipping and distribution – an integrated industry that is the powerhouse of Abu Dhabi's economy. One indication of the importance of the industry is the amount being spent on expansion and upgrading. During the year 2000 alone, some US$6 billion was estimated to have been spent.

Another major component of Abu Dhabi's burgeoning oil-and-gas industry is the Abu Dhabi-controlled Dolphin project, which emerged out of the fertile think-tank of the UAE Offsets Group. Dolphin's basic objective is to transport gas from Qatar's huge offshore field to a landfall near Taweela

and then on to Dubai, and eventually, it is hoped, to other countries in the region, making Abu Dhabi the centre of a new regional network.

The availability of the gas, it is believed, will stimulate massive investment in industry. The cost of the first phase of Dolphin is estimated at around US$3.5 billion, although the total network could cost as much as US$10 billion.

## Effects on the environment

The oil and gas industry recognises a responsibility to the future of Abu Dhabi extending beyond that of simply providing the financial resources that underpin and make possible its continued growth.

In the early phases of the discovery and development of the fields – and then of the massive growth that saw Adnoc emerge as one of the largest integrated oil and gas producers in the world – the main priority was growth itself. One consequence was that, in Abu Dhabi as elsewhere, the oil industry was responsible for a significant degree of environmental pollution. In the deserts and offshore, cast-aside equipment had left its mark, while the flaring of associated gas from the oilfields had a massive, if largely unrecognised, impact on the atmosphere.

The picture began to change in the mid-1970s.

*Environmental organisations have attracted the long-term support of Abu Dhabi's oil companies.*

The value of natural gas as a clean fuel began to be widely recognised, and it became apparent that the flaring represented not simply the burning of a depletable resource, but the burning of money as well.

At the same time, there was the gradual emergence at a global level of a greater degree of environmental consciousness. Abu Dhabi was not immune. The UAE's first voluntary environmental organisation, the Emirates Natural History Group, was formed in 1977, and promptly attracted long-term support from the oil companies, a relationship that continues today.

During the last few years, the Adnoc group has devised and implemented one of the toughest environmental protection programmes found in the oil industry. Millions of dollars have been spent on cleaning up the waste from a previous, less enlightened period, while the flaring of natural gas has been steadily reduced. A target has now been set of a 'zero-flare policy' within the next few years.

The maturity of Abu Dhabi's oil industry has also meant that many of the older installations, particularly offshore, are reaching the end of their working life. As part of a campaign to rehabilitate the seabed, rigs, well-heads and production platforms scheduled for de-commissioning are now being converted into artificial reefs where fish can safely breed. All this is expensive, of course, but these moves are not only important in terms of their environmental impact, but are also necessary for the development of the industry.

Adnoc has shown that it is also prepared to make a direct choice between development of oil production and conservation of the environment. In the mid-1990s, serious consideration was given to the possible development of the offshore Hair Dalma field, west of Abu Dhabi, first discovered more than 20 years earlier. New wells were drilled, and plans were drawn up to bring it into production. The oil reservoirs, however, had associated gases that could not be utilised and had the potential to cause severe atmospheric pollution. After millions of dollars had been spent, the plan to develop the field was shelved on environmental grounds.

Another example of the commitment of Abu Dhabi's oil industry to the environment also comes from offshore. Studies of atmospheric emissions in the late 1990s showed that around 70 per cent of the emissions came from a few small offshore fields. One field, Arzanah, was shut down.

In the others, operated by the Abu Dhabi Oil Company (Japan), a multi-million dollar programme for the reinjection of sour and acid gas was imple-

*Clearing old equipment and a zero-flare policy has allowed the desert to return to its natural splendour.*

mented. As a result, not only has flaring of emissions been virtually eliminated, but the rate of oil recovery from the field has increased, evidence that a responsible environmental approach can have a profitable outcome as well.

As the economy of Abu Dhabi, and the UAE as a whole, has continued to expand and diversify, so the oil sector's share of the GDP has continued to decline. In excess of two thirds in the 1970s, it has fallen through the years to less than a third for the country as a whole and to around a half for Abu Dhabi, by far the largest oil producer. Although its contribution varies because of the vagaries of international oil prices, the underlying trend remains firmly downwards.

Yet it remains central to the economy, partly because of the employment, construction and engineering projects related to it but, more crucially, because it continues to provide the bulk of the income received by the government, which is then spent on other sectors throughout the economy. This will continue in the years ahead.

## Chapter Six

# A green and pleasant Emirate

A first-time visitor to the Emirate of Abu Dhabi may well arrive with a mental image of miles of rolling, barren sand dunes, interspersed with only the occasional oasis of palm trees. Such an impression can be forgiven for, after all, Abu Dhabi does lie in desert Arabia, on the edge of the great Rub al-Khali, or 'Empty Quarter', one of the most arid environments on earth.

This image, though, was never completely accurate, and is today far from true. During the last three

*The results of extensive agricultural development in the Emirate (above) contrast with the natural desert landscape of rolling, barren sand dunes.*

*Abu Dhabi city has numerous parks and gardens.*

*Water still runs through an old* falaj *water-channel.*

decades, Abu Dhabi has seen the implementation of one of the world's most extensive programmes of afforestation and agricultural development, with considerably more than 100-million trees, and a further 40 million or so date palms, being planted across the desert, covering an area of around 200,000 hectares.

At the same time, the major urban centres have been well-supplied with lavish parks and gardens, 25 in the city of Abu Dhabi alone, while rows of trees line the highways through the desert, providing both a touch of green against the sandy coloured wastes, and shelter belts to hold back the movement of the shifting sands.

It is little wonder then that the city of Abu Dhabi itself has earned the nickname 'Garden City of the Gulf', and that the Emirate as a whole now manages to grow millions of tonnes of vegetables and fodder on what was once nothing but arid sand flats or gravel plains.

In a place such as Abu Dhabi, where rainfall is scanty and unpredictable and where there's not a single natural stream or river, it's not surprising that one of the dreams of its people has been that of waving fields of crops, of forests and gardens and lush greenery that nature itself does not provide. During the last 35 years or so, great strides have been made towards turning that dream into reality.

The driving force behind the afforestation-and-agricultural programme, as with so many other aspects of the Emirate's development, has been Sheikh Zayed. Brought up partly in the inland oasis of Al Ain, he became Ruler's Representative there in 1946, marking the beginning of what has now been considerably more than half a century in government.

One of his earliest tasks was to revive agriculture in the area. He achieved that partly by arranging for some of the old *aflaj* (underground water channels) to be cleaned out and repaired so they would flow again, a process in which he took part himself, crawling along the tunnels with his people. He also arranged for a new *falaj* to be dug, the first in many years.

Furthermore, in an early example of his determination to ensure that resources were shared, he revised the ancient system of water distribution and ordered that henceforth farmers in the oasis should have access to the water they needed without charge. Not surprisingly, the agricultural sector of Al Ain's economy promptly took a turn for the better.

At the same time, Sheikh Zayed also deliberately set out to plan for the long-term beautification of what, at the time, was nothing more than a cluster of six little villages of mud-brick houses surrounded by

*Abu Dhabi has a number of decorative fountains which enhance its green areas.*

*With its lavish parks and gardens, it's not for nothing that Abu Dhabi is called the 'Garden City of the Gulf'.*

*Another of the water features that are a common sight in Abu Dhabi parks.*

palm groves and scrub. During the 1950s, he commenced the planting of tender saplings along the edges of dusty sandy tracks, arranging for them to be individually watered every day. Today those saplings are great avenues of trees, lining the modern highways of the city of Al Ain and making it one of the greenest in Arabia.

## Afforestation

When Sheikh Zayed became Ruler of Abu Dhabi in 1966, the tree planting he had initiated in Al Ain spread, at first slowly, and then explosively, to cover the whole of the Emirate. Out in the deserts, once home to only the occasional hardy *ghaf*, or acacia, vast areas are covered by tree plantations, some relatively small while others cover hundreds or even thousands of hectares – serried ranks of vegetation stretching away as far as the eye can see.

Amid the modern buildings of the cities and towns, well-planted parks offer 'green lungs' that would be the envy of many other countries. They are not merely relaxing to the eye but also provide venues for leisure and recreation that are eagerly sought after, especially during the cooler months of the year. It has, by any standards, been a truly remarkable achievement.

The process of afforestation and the reclamation of land for agriculture has been given a significant boost in recent years by the ready availability of desalinated water, a by-product of electricity generation. At the same time, however, in an effort to ensure that wastage is kept to a minimum, virtually all the sewage and other waste water from the city of Abu Dhabi is recycled, producing some 200,000 cubic metres of treated water a day. This is then used for irrigation not only of the city's parks and gardens, but also for other schemes such as the large fodder fields at Al Wathba Camel Track, 40 kilometres east of the city.

A similar concern for the conservation of valuable freshwater resources can be seen in many of the desert plantations, where pipelines have been laid for tens of kilometres in order to bring desalinated or recycled water to the trees.

Contrary to the popular but erroneously held image of the United Arab Emirates as a wholly desert country, the Emirate of Abu Dhabi has always had some agriculture. In the Al Ain Oasis, the tapping of underground resources by wells and, since around 1,000 BC, by *aflaj* has permitted farming for at least 5,000 years, while in the great arc of the Liwa Oasis in the south, small palm groves have always been able to survive, thanks to the trapping of underground reservoirs of fresh water at the base of the great sand-dunes.

Now, however, agricultural production has expanded, thanks to the ready availability of goverment assistance for farmers. Such assistance can include the preparation of farm land, the drilling of water wells or laying of pipes to bring desalinated water, and then the handing-over, completely free of charge, of a farm ready for cultivation.

The help continues, with the provision of seeds and fertilisers at a subsidised rate, and a guaranteed government purchase scheme for crops for those farmers who wish to take advantage of it. Not surprisingly, the growth in agricultural production has been substantial. By the year 2000, more than 20,000 farms had been established, covering nearly 658,000 *dunams* (acres) of land, around 60 per cent of it in the Eastern Region around Al Ain, and the rest near Abu Dhabi city and in the Western Region. By way of contrast, in 1996, there were 12,315 farms, covering just 414,000 *dunams*. More are prepared every year.

More than 2.2 million tonnes of vegetables are now produced annually, with a value in excess of Dhs3.5 billion, an impressive total for an agricultural sector that can rarely count upon the blessing of rainfall. The main crops are salad vegetables, the most

*Most of the UAE's dates grow in Abu Dhabi.*

*Dates, once part of the staple diet of the area, are still a popular treat – especially during Ramadan.*

**Al Ain's green landscape amply demonstrates the success of tree planting.**

popular being tomatoes and cabbages, although other crops such as potatoes have also been successfully introduced following extensive field trials by government agricultural research stations.

The country is now one of the largest producers of dates in the world, with more than 40 million date palms having been planted in the UAE as a whole, the vast majority of them in Abu Dhabi. Some of the dates themselves are for the farmers' own consumption, while several thousand tonnes a year are processed and packed for local supermarkets or export. In the towns and cities, dates on trees by the roadside or in the parks can be freely collected and eaten by anyone.

Animal husbandry has not been neglected, with total livestock at the end of 2000 consisting of nearly 230,000 camels, nearly a million goats and sheep and some 19,500 cattle, of which 6,500 were in modern dairy farms. Poultry farms, with their intensive programme of food production, produce nearly 1,200-million eggs a year.

It is, of course, unlikely that the UAE will ever produce all the food it needs. Experiments with crops such as wheat have shown that the yield per hectare is very low, quite apart from the expense of production, while the climate is simply not conducive to the growing of some crops. There is now also concern that grazing by sheep and goats is having an adverse impact on the fragile plant life of the desert regions.

The results of agricultural experimentation and of the afforestation programme show clearly, however, that much can be achieved provided that the water, investment and, above all, the determination is there.

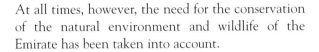
*Bougainvillaea is a firm favourite in the Emirate.*

At all times, however, the need for the conservation of the natural environment and wildlife of the Emirate has been taken into account.

## Natural environment

To the casual observer, it may seem as though Abu Dhabi's natural environment is relatively uninteresting. There may be sand dunes, salt flats and coastal beaches with occasional stands of mangroves, but there are certainly no great natural forests or endless prairies. The climate, of course, precludes this and plant and animal life has to struggle to survive in the harsh desert and semi-desert. Indeed, the very nature of this environment means that the survival of wildlife is often precarious, and even a limited amount of human impact can have a devastating effect.

However, the surface geology of Abu Dhabi, in effect the scenery itself, has a beauty of its own, while it is also of considerable scientific interest. The *sabkha* (salt flats), which stretch from northeast of Abu Dhabi all along the coastline to the Sila'a area in the extreme west, are the largest of their kind in the world, and have provided geological information of international importance.

Some can also be found far inland. The great sand-dunes of the Liwa area reach up to 100 metres high, with inter-dunal gravel or *sabkha* lying between them. Comprising the northeast edge of the Empty Quarter, they are also important examples of the type. Anyone who has seen the dunes in the dawn or dusk light will be able to testify that they can, indeed, have a beauty

*The beautiful clear water off the shores of Abu Dhabi.*

ago. In the waters of the Arabian Gulf, several species of turtle and dolphin and the endangered dugong, or 'sea-cow,' can be found, as well as an occasional whale for the lucky observer.

## Wildlife protection

Within the landscape and seascape is a multitude of fascinating wildlife, much of it being the object of study both by the Environment Research and Wildlife Development Agency (Erwda), a government body, and by members of voluntary organisations such as the Emirates Natural History Group, now 25 years old, and the Emirates Bird Records Committee, which maintains the official list of bird species seen in the country.

With HH Sheikh Khalifa bin Zayed Al Nahyan, Crown Prince and Deputy Supreme Commander of the UAE Armed Forces as its Chairman, and Minister of State for Foreign Affairs HE Sheikh Hamdan bin Zayed Al Nahyan as its Deputy Chairman, Erwda is charged with both studying and protecting the wildlife of the Emirate – not just the

and grandeur all their own.

The only real mountain within the territory of Abu Dhabi, the great whaleback of Jebel Hafit, just south of Al Ain, which rises to around 1,000 metres above sea level, has been carved by the forces of nature through millions of years into often fantastical shapes, while fossils millions of years old can be found amid its rocks.

From its top, you can look out for miles over the city of Al Ain or out across the adjacent deserts on a clear day. Deep inside the mountain are long caves carved out by water action in the past, although these are inaccessible except with special permission.

The coasts and islands of the Emirate have their own importance, although most of the latter are off-limits to casual visitors, while offshore on the seabed there are millions of pearl oysters, harvested for thousands of years by local inhabitants until a few decades plants and animals but, importantly, also the surrounding environment in which they live.

The agency is, for example, studying the gentle dugong, a marine mammal said to be the origin of the mermaid legend. In addition, it has also launched a study into marine turtles, involving plotting their nesting sites on offshore islands and tagging some turtles and sailfish with small transmitters so their movements can be tracked by satellite.

Onshore, Erwda and scientists from other organisations are engaged in studying the plants of the desert and some of the animals that live among them, such as the desert hare, of which at least two subspecies are present, and a host of lizards and smaller animals. A key focus of their work is the study of the houbara bustard, the favoured quarry of local falconers, and of saker and peregrine falcons. One of the objectives is to develop a captive-breeding programme as part of the efforts to conserve all three species in the wild.

Erwda is also responsible for the designation and management of protected areas, in association with the Abu Dhabi Islands Archaeological Survey (Adias), which is charged with responsibility for archaeological and fossil sites on the coast and islands of the Emirate. The first protected marine area, covering more than 4,000 square kilometres of inshore waters around the island of Marawah, as well as the island itself and other smaller islands, was formally designated early in 2002.

Among the most easily conspicuous wildlife in Abu Dhabi is the bird population. Studies by members of the Emirates Bird Records Committee and other ornithologists have shown that more than 100 species of birds breed in the Emirates, many of them in Abu Dhabi. Offshore islands such as Qarnein, Yasat al-Ulya and Dayyinah, for example, are home during the summer breeding season to colonies of thousands of sea birds.

Qarnein, granted special protection by Sheikh Hamdan bin Zayed, is one of the most important sites for breeding birds anywhere in the whole of Arabia. It has now been designated as a 'Gift to the Earth' under

*Mangroves – an important ecosystem – are a common sight along the Abu Dhabi coastline.*

*A sand gazelle on the island sanctuary of Sir Bani Yas, created by Sheikh Zayed.*

a programme designed by the Worldwide Fund for Nature, WWF, to preserve some of the world's best nature reserves for all time.

Besides the breeding birds, there are the passage migrants, hundreds of thousands of which pass through Abu Dhabi every year during their migration from breeding grounds in Siberia to wintering grounds in Africa. Tens of thousands of birds choose to overwinter in Abu Dhabi, and key wetland sites such as the Dabb'iya Peninsula and the island of Marawah, west of Abu Dhabi, or the Al Wathba Lakes (an Erwda-managed nature sanctuary around 40 kilometres inland from Abu Dhabi), can, at their peak, hold several thousand birds.

Even in the city itself there are important sites for birds, such as the mangrove-lined Eastern Lagoon on the eastern side of the island, important for sea birds and waders, and the Ra's al-Akhdar headland at the northwestern tip, which regularly produces rare species of migrants and also has a number of breeding species.

During the last few years, the UAE has begun to attract visitors from overseas who come with the specific intention of looking at the country's varied birdlife: of the 420 or so species recorded in the UAE, more than 75 per cent have been seen on the island of Abu Dhabi itself. It is probable that no other major city in the world can offer such a large percentage of a country's bird list.

Conservation of the environment, both on land and offshore, and of the wildlife to be found within it, has long been a part of government policy. Hunting of wildlife was, for example, banned throughout the Emirate in 1977, while under the terms of more recent legislation, no major projects may be undertaken without a proper study being made of the likely impact on the environment, wildlife and aspects of cultural heritage such as archaeological sites, this study then being subject to vetting and approval by Erwda.

The moving force behind the policy is President Sheikh Zayed, who has led the way by creating an impressive collection of endxangered wildlife on the western island of Sir Bani Yas. Its focus is on species indigenous to the UAE, such as the Arabian oryx and sand and mountain gazelles, and those native to other desert and semi-desert areas, such as the scimitar-horned oryx and the addax. The latter two species are both from Africa and are seriously endangered, if not extinct, in the wild, so the collection is of international importance.

Release programmes for Arabian oryx and both sand and mountain gazelles have been started in the desert regions of Abu Dhabi, and the lucky explorer venturing

*Marine turtles' movements are closely monitored.*

out into the remoter regions may well be rewarded with a glimpse of these animals, which once roamed free in large numbers through the desert landscape.

Much of the country's landscape and wildlife is difficult to access or hard to see, although some is easy to visit and simple to spot, whether it be in and around the cities of Abu Dhabi and Al Ain, or from the highways that traverse the desert. Those who keep their eyes open will swiftly find the whole of the Emirate of Abu Dhabi a fascinating and remarkable place.

*A group of lesser crested terns on Qarnein Island.*

## Chapter Seven

# The leisure industry

THERE HAS BEEN A TREMENDOUS GROWTH IN WESTERN-style sports and leisure activities since oil first started flowing from Abu Dhabi's wells in the early 1960s. This growth was caused by the large influx of expatriates and the great interest shown by the local population in non-traditional sports. The upshot was an astonishing range and quality of sports facilities equal to any other in the world. The booming leisure industry benefits from almost perfect weather conditions for nearly eight months of the year – as well as some high disposable incomes.

Nevertheless, traditional Arabian sports have not been forgotten and, with the encouragement of Sheikh Zayed, who has always stressed the importance of the nation's heritage, many have indeed flourished.

Falconry and camel racing, for example, have always been linked to the Gulf states. Before the discovery of oil, these two activities were deeply rooted in the indigenous way of life, but both activities have

*Left: Abu Dhabi has perfect beach weather for most of the year. Above: Fishing is another popular leisure option, with some exciting catches to be had.*

*Jubilant football fans at Sheikh Zayed Sports City. Football is the most popular national sport.*

now become full-fledged sports in their own right. Although falcons are no longer used except for sport, falconry is still a dominant symbol of national cultural identity and is becoming more popular with local enthusiasts.

The Arabian dromedary, once an essential means of transport for the Bedouins and today largely replaced by 4x4s, is still commonly used in camel races. The one-humped camel remains a source of pride for owners who partake in races, a common widespread attraction on Thursdays and Fridays during the cooler months. Considerable time and money is invested in these animals and winners may be as pampered as racing Thoroughbred horses.

There is much friendly rivalry among camel owners, and big prizes are at stake. Spectators are guaranteed a memorable experience, particularly since the owners cruise alongside the racetrack in their 4x4s beside their galloping entries, adding to the busy, colourful atmosphere.

Abu Dhabi's history is linked not only to the desert but also to the sea – a tie still widely celebrated on national and religious holidays with picturesque sailing and rowing races off the Abu Dhabi Corniche or Al Raha Beach near Maqta Bridge.

The rowing races on such occasions are not to be missed, if only to admire the beauty of the dark, slender boats gliding through the turquoise waters and hear the chanting of the oarsmen. Rowers arrive from all over the Emirates to compete both for cash prizes and for the honour of their team. Each traditional hand-made teak boat, between 40 and 60 feet in length, is manned by between 70 and 150 oarsmen, and the preparations and post-race celebrations themselves are colourful spectacles of local traditions.

Contrary to most people's predictions, the sailing dhow hasn't vanished from local waters and is even enjoying a period of renaissance, albeit for reasons of leisure rather than trade. There can be few more thrilling sights than to watch an elegant full-sized *boom* (as the large trading dhow is known) cresting the waves, with its white hoisted sails billowed by strong winds, competing in the annual regattas.

But other more modern sports also enjoy their share of popularity. The International Marine Sports Club on the Abu Dhabi breakwater has become a leading centre for Formula One Offshore powerboat racing. The international season runs from February to December and ends with a final round hosted in Abu Dhabi. The UAE is represented by the Emirates

A UIM Class Two powerboat from the prizewinning Victory Team shows its paces during a race organised by the Abu Dhabi International Marine Sports Club.

*Abu Dhabi has hosted many international polo teams and is a major contributor to the domestic circuit.*

*Fishing for hammour, red snapper, barracuda, kingfish and sailfish is a perfect way to spend a day off Abu Dhabi.*

Formula One Team, the first and only team from the Arab world to participate in Formula One races.

It was not always so. Thirty years ago, when virtually the only expatriates in Abu Dhabi were those involved in oil exploration, sports facilities were negligible. But once the oil boom took off, both government and private sectors were quick to respond to the need for a leisure industry. Today all the major oil companies have their own sports facilities.

Sheikh Zayed also gave land and support for the construction of major sports outlets and clubs, and under his patronage hotel chains were encouraged to set up in Abu Dhabi and provide further venues tailored primarily to the expatriate community.

The spectacular Zayed Sports City on the Western Road is a measure of Sheikh Zayed's commitment to providing the best facilities for the country's youth, its huge vaulted silhouette housing the latest facilities for football and other major sports events. As in most parts of the world, football is the most popular national sport – particularly among local youths. The participation of the UAE in World Cup finals has given the sport a tremendous boost and the country boasts a thriving league and cup competition in which Abu Dhabi clubs dominate.

The Abu Dhabi Cricket Council's modern 15 million dollar stadium is another example of the Emirate's determination to become a global sporting capital.

For a large number of Abu Dhabians, and for the ever-increasing number of tourists, most leisure activities, especially water sports, are centred around the city's hotels. The major hotels – managed mainly by international chains under the direction of either the Abu Dhabi National Hotels Company or the National Corporation for Tourism and Hotels – are all equipped with extensive recreational club facilities and private beaches.

The climate of Abu Dhabi, with only a few days in midwinter being marred by stormy weather and rain, is ideal for outdoor sports of all types. The spring and autumn months, in particular, promise comfortable temperatures ranging from 20°C to 30°C and water sports, especially windsurfing with the good winds and calm waters in the Abu Dhabi Bay, have flourished in recent years. Jet-skiing (particularly fashionable among young locals), water-skiing and diving are also popular. Sailing enthusiasts, too, have a wide choice, although smaller dinghy sailing has largely been eclipsed by the excitement of more speedy catamarans.

The Inter-Continental Hotel and Abu Dhabi Marina & Yacht Club both have modern marinas, resplendent with motor launches and yachts of every size and description. The sheltered waters and surrounding islands make Abu Dhabi a safe and exciting

*Tennis courts are not difficult to find in the capital and there are many tournaments for all levels and ages.*

81

*Although certain driving skills are obviously necessary, dune driving is a widespread leisure pursuit.*

playground for powerboat enthusiasts, many of whom own their own speedboats.

During the weekends water-skiers and anglers take to the seas in droves – fishing for local *hammour*, red snapper, kingfish and sailfish is a perfect way to spend a day – while other people prefer to explore or picnic on the many islands. Dhows are available for hire by the half-day, full day or evening, and barbecues on the beach are a favourite alternative to indoor parties.

Many leading hotels, including Le Meridien, Sheraton Resort & Towers, Inter-Continental and the Beach Rotana Hotel have temperature-controlled swimming pools and provide swimming lessons with trained instructors. Scuba-diving lessons are also available, leading to internationally-recognised certification such as those of the Padi (Professional Association of Diving Instructors) organisation.

In a constant battle to outdo each other, the recreation and health clubs offer an astonishing array of sports and leisure opportunities, ranging from paragliding and banana-boat rides to squash and salsa classes. Gymnasiums are fully equipped with state-of-the-art exercise machines and offer training courses such as weight loss or bodybuilding, all under the supervision of qualified instructors. Those seeking a more relaxed approach can sink into a Jacuzzi, soak in a sauna or steam room, or take in some shiatsu or Chinese massage, followed by an aromatherapy session.

Abu Dhabi is a tremendous place to take up a new hobby or sport, as various clubs offer classes as diverse as horse-riding, karate, ballet, t'ai chi, jazz dance and aerobics.

Tennis, the perfect social game, continues to be a favourite pastime, with many tournaments and competitions for all levels and ages. The Abu Dhabi Health and Fitness Club even runs its own tennis academy, and floodlit courts make it possible to play

*The Arabian Gulf is a good place to learn diving skills.*

in the relative cool of the summer evenings. Another popular racquet sport, particularly during the hot and humid summer months, is squash, played on air-conditioned courts.

Not all clubs are based in hotels, however: there are many clubs for the different nationalities among the expatriate labour force and larger, more established companies often provide recreational facilities for their employees. One of the oldest, independent establishments is known simply as The Club, sometimes erroneously referred to as the British Club, although it attracts members of every nationality for its social, sporting and cultural activities The Abu Dhabi Marina & Yacht Club has also become a popular venue among expatriates as well as well-travelled visitors.

The Tourist Club, which gives its name to the

*Golfers are able to enjoy a game both on grass or on traditional sand courses in Abu Dhabi.*

A number of adventure travel companies offer exciting guided safaris into the desert.

Desert trips may include a barbeque, a camel ride, smoking shisha, belly-dancing and even a night under canvas.

area stretching from the Meridien to the International Hotel, is popular among families and boasts Abu Dhabi's only go-karting course and a 10-pin bowling centre, while the ice-skating rink at Zayed Sports City can accommodate 450 skaters and 1,200 spectators, and is the regular venue for local and expatriate ice-hockey teams.

One of the newest equestrian facilities is that at Ghantoot, home of the Ghantoot Racing & Polo Club. The first floodlit polo club in Abu Dhabi Emirate, it's hosted many international teams and has become a major contributor to the domestic polo circuit.

Foremost among desert activities has to be off-road driving, where motoring enthusiasts head out in 4x4 vehicles to explore the desert and mountain wilderness. For those who don't want to venture out in their own vehicles, the major car-hire companies are all well supplied with 4x4s for weekend expeditions. Novices are advised always to travel in convoys, as it's easy to get stuck in the soft sand or lost in the desert. For those who feel happier in the hands of professionals, a number of adventure travel companies offer guided desert safaris. Such trips may include an Arabian barbecue, a camel ride, smoking *shisha*, belly dancing and even a night under canvas.

As a direct offshoot of these desert safaris, sand-skiing was introduced as an exhilarating sport on the splendid reddish dunes of Liwa Oasis and Al Ain, reputed to be among the tallest in the world. A 4x4 is often used to ferry the skiers back to the summit of the steep dunes.

On a less slippery and more genteel note, there is golf. Traditionally, the game here was played on sand but, in order to simulate the grass game as much as possible, players hit the ball off a piece of Astroturf – except on the compacted sand greens, better known as 'browns'. But in the past few years, the Abu Dhabi Golf & Equestrian Club and the Abu Dhabi Golf Club by Sheraton have introduced world-class, all-grass putting 'greens' and floodlit driving ranges to match international circuit standards.

Whether you enjoy chess, quilting, bird-watching or classical music, there's also a full quota of social, cultural and natural-history clubs and societies. One of the most active is the Emirates Natural History Group, whose programme includes regular talks on local wildlife, geology and archaeology as well as outings.

As the capital city, Abu Dhabi regularly attracts top international entertainers, from world-famous pop stars to the Russian State Ballet Company. International festivals range from Scandinavian promotions to a Rio Carnival, while the annual Al Ain

*Sand-skiing was introduced as a direct offshoot of desert safaris in the dunes near Liwa Oasis and Al Ain.*

Music Festival attracts more and more music lovers every year.

The Abu Dhabi Cultural Foundation organises an impressive variety of less commercial events. Located in 14 hectares of lush gardens, this modern complex – designed in traditional Arabian style – holds a wide range of art exhibitions, concerts, plays, lectures, movie screenings, film festivals and poetry readings. Art workshops, language courses, children's activities and an annual book fair are also offered.

Introducing the cultural life of the capital without mentioning its wonderful variety of restaurants would be quite unforgivable. In the many cafés or hotel restaurants around town, there are dishes to satisfy all palates, including cuisines from around the world, seafood and themed buffets. Belly dancing in the Oriental restaurants and clubs, or live jazz in the major hotel lounges, is another part of the regular entertainment. For a quieter evening, dinner on one of the floating dhow restaurants is sure to be a memorable choice.

An up-to-date listing of restaurants, cinemas, clubs, activities and contacts can be found each month in the pages of *What's On* magazine.

## Chapter Eight

# The world on display

A BU DHABI OFFERS AN ARRAY OF GOODS FROM ALL over the world, in shops that range from designer boutiques to open-air stalls. Shoppers in the city quickly discover an astonishing choice that combines old and new. There is the pleasure of exploring the malls, department stores, boutiques and souks, with the bonus of a superb variety of products and competitive prices – indeed, prices for many imported luxury goods are cheaper than in their country of origin.

## Traditional souks

The Middle Eastern souk, or market-place, has an ambience uniquely its own, reminiscent of another era. Like voyagers of the past, today's travellers can still find perfumes, jewellery, silks, spices, nuts and dried fruits beside cheap trinkets, plastic sandals and electronic toys. Bargaining over prices is customary, especially in the souks, and can be a way of practicing your Arabic and improving your negotiating skills. Many visitors remember this as a highlight of their trip. To avoid embarrassment, however, remember that in the plusher showrooms and boutiques, prices are usually fixed!

Abu Dhabi's main souk is at the top end of Sheikh Hamdan Street and extends all the way to Sheikh Khalifa Street. This souk consists of an open, central pedestrian avenue leading into a large main square. On either side is an interconnected grid of narrow walkways, interspersed with several smaller squares. The overhead walkway leads to the Old Souk, on the

*Abu Dhabi offers a wonderful array of goods from all over the world, in shops that range from up-market designer boutiques to simple stalls in souks.*

*A wide range of local and imported fresh fruit and vegetables is on display.*

*Abu Dhabi's souks offer an interesting variety of local, Arab and other goods.*

opposite side of Sheikh Khalifa Street, which stretches almost all the way to the Corniche. This entire area is crammed with small shops and stalls selling a diverse assortment of goods: gold, watches, household appliances, clothes, mattresses, shoes, material, *shishas*, incense and Arab artefacts.

The new fish-and-vegetable souk is located between Istiqlal and Al Nasr streets. This beautiful structure, inspired by traditional Islamic architecture, incorporates the best in modern facilities and design. Fresh fish, meat and produce are all available under one air-conditioned roof, making it convenient to shop for *hammour* (grouper), chicken or exotic fruits and vegetables. For those taking their cameras along, note that it is always best to ask before taking somebody's photograph, and to avoid photographing women.

Smaller neighbourhood souks are scattered throughout the city, including one arched pavilion off Mina Road, known as the Afghani Souk, that sells carpets, mattresses and pillows for the traditional *majlis* in addition to household goods. Apart from a few small hand-made rugs from Afghanistan, the carpets here are all machine-made, mass-produced copies of old patterns and styles and therefore reasonably priced. Bargaining is nonetheless recommended.

A little further away, at the Dhow Harbour, the

*Coffee pots are popular mementoes.*

Iranian Souk offers everything from plants, hand-painted tiles, terracotta pots, kilims and kitchenware to furniture. The nearby air-conditioned fish market overflows with daily arrivals of local seafood, includ-

*Pottery, an age-old craft, is still a firm favourite with tourists.*

*Abu Dhabi's souks sell a wide variety of goods that cater for all ages and tastes.*

*At Abu Dhabi's Gold Centre, gold jewellery is sold by weight, at prices much lower than in the West.*

ing shark and barracuda, and the open-air stalls of the fruit-and-vegetable souk bustle with shoppers and vendors auctioning crates of colourful produce.

Visitors to Abu Dhabi's souks often take home with them far more than their souvenirs – they take a lasting memory of local hospitality and atmosphere, and a time-honoured way of life that lives on even in today's modern society.

More conventional shopping can be found along and between the three main streets: Sheikh Zayed the Second, Sheikh Hamdan and Sheikh Khalifa, all running parallel to each other and to Abu Dhabi's scenic Corniche. The range of goods on offer is an eclectic combination of past and present. For antique collectors, there are magnificent Arab chests, long the most prominent piece of furniture in Gulf homes. Made of teakwood with solid brass handles, decorated with copper studs and ornate mother-of-pearl inlays, these genuine dowry chests, called *mendoos*, were traditionally presented to a girl by her father when she became engaged and were used for storing clothes and jewellery. Many have drawers in the bot-

90

*Carpets from Iran, Afghanistan and other countries are sold in traditional souks and modern shopping malls.*

tom or secret compartments. Authentic antique *mendoos* are now eagerly sought and expensive.

Copper and brass coffee pots, known in Arabic as *dalla*, are also indispensable to the Arab way of life, and have been for centuries. A small, strong cup of coffee is generally served after meals and to every visitor to your home or place of business. The coffee pot is an appropriate cultural emblem on the one-dirham coin. Antique coffee pots are in great demand and can be found in a variety of styles depending on their region of origin, but all have the characteristic long, curved, beak-like spout. An old pot in reasonably good condition can command a high price.

Other popular traditional items are the *khanjar*, the short, curved steel dagger in a finely-etched sheath that, until recently, was carried on a belt by every man in the region; old rifles, some decorated with silver inlays; falconry accoutrements such as hoods or decorative perches; and relics of the pearling industry – the curved knives used by the divers in the past are quite rare – and the prized Gulf pearls themselves that are still found from time to time in local shops.

Bedouin jewellery, typically heavy, chunky pieces in silver, often combined with semi-precious stones, is particularly striking. Bedouin women traditionally received their first set when they married: bracelets, necklaces, rings for fingers and toes, belts, earrings, medallions and amulets. The silver used in making these pieces used to be obtained by melting down Maria Theresa dollars, formerly the accepted currency throughout the Gulf.

When budgets do not stretch to antiques, there is a wide range of more modest souvenirs and handicrafts to choose from, including replica coffee pots and miniature coffee sets, brass camels, trays and incense burners.

## Modern shopping

With the arrival of Abu Dhabi's two new malls, shopping in the capital attracts all the more attention. Located in the Tourist Club area, the Abu Dhabi Mall is one of the largest in the UAE. The huge Dhs 510 million complex, part of the Abu Dhabi Trade Centre, houses more than 200 shops and stores, and reflects Abu Dhabi's international standards with such various retail names as Max Mara, Mont Blanc, Pierre Cardin, The Body Shop and Virgin Megastore.

Shoppers can find everything from affordable fashions and exclusive designer labels and accessories to gifts, jewellery, digital cameras, video equipment and music – and they're also treated to a fine selection of coffee shops and restaurants.

The Marina Mall, set at the Breakwater overlooking the capital's impressive skyline, promises a different shopping, entertainment and leisure experience. With its landmark rooftop, the Marina Mall is a shopper's paradise, offering major international chains such as Ikea and Carrefour as well as some 150 shops and boutiques. It also features one of the largest multiplex cinemas in the UAE and a unique metallic fountain that can emulate rain and fog, synchronized to the background music.

The Madinat Zayed Shopping and Gold Centre on Muroor Road is another large city mall with its own special attractions. Divided into two huge but elegant buildings, each topped by three domes, it is a vast retail complex and gold centre. The latter is an excellent place to bargain for items of exquisite craftsmanship, sold by weight at prices much lower than in the West. The former is particularly well supplied with

fabrics – sequinned gauzes, gold-threaded brocades, iridescent silks from Japan, raw silks from India and flowery organdies in rich glowing tones, delicate pastels and shimmering golds and silvers.

For those after gift shops, there are a number around Abu Dhabi selling exquisite crystal, silver, leather goods, china and porcelain figurines imported from all over the world. Lalique, Bernardaud, Daum, Baccarat, Limoges, Dupont and Christofle are some of the famous European names for glassware, crystal and china in the capital's more exclusive boutiques.

Designer clothes for women and men are not in short supply either: Yves Saint Laurent, Dior and Nina Ricci from Paris; Hugo Boss from Germany; Giorgio Armani from Italy; and Ralph Lauren from America – to name a few – can be found around town in the various luxury boutiques. Plenty of lower-priced fashion stores such as Benetton, British Home Stores, Marks & Spencer and Next operate under franchises, and there are scores of shops selling cotton casuals from the Indian subcontinent.

Art shops often sell prints, watercolours or pen-and-ink drawings of local scenes, many painted by expatriate artists who have been inspired by the heritage, landscape and wildlife of the Emirates. On a practical level, it is worth pointing out that the local

*This impressive fountain is the centrepiece of the Marina Mall.*

*Shoppers enjoy a quiet moment next to the Marina Mall's fountain.*

*From exotic Bedouin jewellery to top-selling toys, Abu Dhabi Duty Free has it all.*

pharmacies are well stocked with the latest pharmaceutical products, as well as toiletries and cosmetics.

Local supermarkets such as Spinneys also offer a huge selection of international foods, whether Oreo cookies, Chinese noodles, Russian caviar or French Brie, in order to satisfy an eclectic international expatriate community. For those with a sweet tooth, pastries in this part of the world may prove irresistible. Arab sweets, made with honey or syrup, stuffed with dates, sprinkled with crushed pistachio nuts, and soaked in rose water, are delicious, especially when accompanied by a traditional glass of tea with mint leaves.

Muffins, croissants, French pastries and nut breads are commonly sold around town in established outlets such as Café du Roi, Starbucks, La Brioche and other such coffee shops.

**The large Abu Dhabi Mall is situated in the popular Tourist Club area of the city.**

## Duty-free shopping

No account of Abu Dhabi's elaborate shopping facilities would be complete without mention of the duty-free complex at Abu Dhabi International Airport. Better known as ADDF, it is one of the best duty frees in the world and internationally recognised for its marketing, quality and innovation. Located in the airport's futuristic, state-of-the-art satellite terminal, its 29 branded shops and corners are spread across some 3,450 square metres of retail space.

Prices are competitively low and customer service

***Abu Dhabi Duty Free, one of the best in the world, is recognised for its marketing quality and innovation.***

is of a high standard. It was the first duty free in the Middle East to implement the 'Brand Name' concept into its shops. Set in a domed concourse decorated with striking Arabian-style hexagonal tiling, there are separate departments for electronic items, local antiques, perfumes, fashion, food, books, watches, jewellery, tobacco, liquor and toys. Brand names include Bally, Calvin Klein, Canon, Cartier, Chanel, Dior, Disney, Gaultier, Givenchy, Rolex, Swatch, Versace and Yves Saint Laurent.

ADDF already covers two floors and has been expanded, with 20 new outlets and branded corners on the upper level. A second satellite terminal is already under construction and should be inaugurated in 2005, more than doubling the duty free area with

an additional 4,000 square metres of retail space. The complex is also famous for its 'Flights of Fortune' promotion that can turn a lucky ticket holder into the owner of a Porsche or Mercedes.

In 1986, Abu Dhabi's duty-free complex was awarded 'Best New Duty Free Shopping Outlet' worldwide at the Duty-Free Symposium in Cannes and won two Frontier Marketing awards in 1986 and 1987. Since then, its excellence has brought further accolades, although the greatest praise comes from passengers, who consistently vote Abu Dhabi's complex one of the best in the world.

*A typical piece of silver Bedouin jewellery would make an ideal souvenir of Abu Dhabi and the UAE.*

# Selected hotels in Abu Dhabi

Abu Dhabi's many fine hotels – a number of them overlooking the Arabian Gulf – rank among the best in the world, with renowned international and local brands ensuring the highest standards and facilities for the visitor. The local market expects first-class international service and the Emirate's leading hotels are geared to meet the most exacting standards. A selection of top hotels follows. . . .

## Abu Dhabi International Airport Hotel
PO Box 3167, Abu Dhabi, UAE
Tel: (+971 2) 575 7377, fax: (+971 2) 575 7458
e-mail: airport@emirates.net.ae   www.abudhabiairporthotel.com

Abu Dhabi International Airport Hotel offers 19 *en suite* rooms; a restaurant; a comfortable lounge with a complimentary bar and massage chairs; a health club equipped with a Nautilus gym, sauna and Jacuzzi; a children's play area; and a business centre with professional secretaries, telephone, fax and Internet. As part of the expansion programme within the airport, the hotel is being enlarged to 40 rooms, along with a duty-free shop, hairdresser, a larger business centre, secure luggage room and a separate 'snoozing' lounge where passengers will be able to rest before their flights and where there'll be a 30-per-cent increase in space.

## Al Diar Gulf Hotel & Resort
PO Box 3766, Abu Dhabi, UAE
Tel: (+971 2) 441 4777, fax: (+971 2) 441 4537
e-mail: adglfhtl@emirates.net.ae   www.aldiarhotels.com

Located on a beautiful beach, 20 kilometres from the airport and close to the city centre and shops, this resort hotel is perfect for pleasure-loving tourists. It incorporates 273 rooms, six suites, 24 self-catering chalets opening on to picturesque gardens and 50 chalets facing the sea. There are six restaurants: the waterfront Palm Beach Restaurant and Oyster Bar, Sheherezade Coffee Shop, Morgana Disco Club, Sports Complex Terrace, Italiana Pizzeria and the Ranch Restaurant. The friendly and efficient service – and the beach, water sports, health club, tennis, squash and other leisure and entertainment facilities – will ensure you enjoy the capital's best-kept secret.

## Al Jazira Hotel & Resort
PO Box 26268, Abu Dhabi, UAE
Tel: (+971 2) 562 9100, fax: (+971 2) 562 9035
e-mail: reservations@jaziraresort.com   www.jaziraresort.com

Situated on the beach, 45 minutes from Abu Dhabi and Dubai, this resort with 80 rooms, four suites and 30 superb chalets, is ideal for family vacations, intimate weekends and day outings. Leisure activities include tennis and squash and there's a sauna and steam bath, gymnasium, swimming pool and children's pool. A private beach offers excellent facilities for water-skiing, sailing, windsurfing, fishing and diving. Guests can enjoy Dalma Restaurant on the beach and the Safina Coffee shop, Lobby Lounge, Bounty English pub, Grillhouse Bar and Checkers nightclub, while conferences, banquets or receptions for 10 to 150 people can be accommodated in a selection of elegant rooms.

## Al Maha Rotana Suites
PO Box 5946, Abu Dhabi, UAE
Tel: (+971 2) 610 6666, fax: (+971 2) 610 6777
e-mail: almaha.suites@rotana.com   www.rotana.com

Al Maha Rotana Suites is in the heart of the main business and shopping district of Abu Dhabi, 10 minutes from the International Exhibition Centre and 30 kilometres from the airport, making it ideal for business and leisure visitors. The 288 luxurious studios and suites offer sea and city views and are fully equipped with kitchenettes, satellite television, mini bar, in-room safe and parking. The banquet rooms accommodate meetings, launches and dinners for up to 120 people. There's also a leisure club, Bodylines, with a fitness centre and swimming pool. The City Café is open all day for breakfast, lunch and dinner.

## Al Rawda Rotana Suites

PO Box 5821, Abu Dhabi, UAE
Tel: (+971 2) 445 7111, fax: (+971 2) 445 7222
e-mail: alrawda.suites@rotana.com   www.rotana.com

Al Rawda Rotana Suites is conveniently situated close to the main commercial, banking and shopping districts of Abu Dhabi and only minutes away from the International Exhibition Centre and some 30 minutes drive from Abu Dhabi International Airport. The 110 deluxe rooms, including 28 suites – among the largest in the island city – are fully equipped with a kitchenette, mini-fridge, satellite television, individual air-conditioning and IDD telephone facilities. The Moka Café is open all day and, in addition to breakfast, lunch and dinner, serves light snacks throughout the day. Room service is also available.

## Beach Rotana Hotel & Towers

PO Box 45200, Abu Dhabi, UAE
Tel: (+971 2) 644 3000, fax: (+971 2) 644 2111
e-mail: beach.hotel@rotana.com   www.rotana.com

Situated in the heart of Abu Dhabi, this property – a member of the Leading Hotels of the World – has 558 sea-facing rooms and suites overlooking a private beach and is linked to the prestigious Abu Dhabi Mall. There are 10 world-class food and beverage venues – each with its own ambience and cuisine. For business guests there's a fully equipped business centre, conference and banqueting facilities, as well as Club Rotana floors for discerning entertaining. Leisure facilities, which will be completed by March 2003, include two swimming pools set in luxurious gardens, a Bodylines leisure and fitness club, a recreation centre, dive centre, two vibrant restaurants and a kids' zone.

## Crowne Plaza Abu Dhabi

PO Box 3541, Abu Dhabi, UAE
Tel: (+971 2) 621 0000, fax: (+971 2) 621 1530
e-mail: reservation@cpauh.co.ae   www.crowneplaza.com

Crowne Plaza Hotel Abu Dhabi is the place where luxury and efficiency go hand in hand to delight business travellers and vacationers alike. Situated in the heart of the city, Crowne Plaza is considered the perfect place for business or pleasure, offering superior facilities coupled with courtesy and luxurious comfort. Guests will enjoy the choice of 236 rooms, including 49 suites and four Executive Floors complete with a business centre and lounge. There are extensive conference and banqueting facilities and six international dining outlets. There's also a newly-refurbished fitness centre and a roof-top swimming pool with breathtaking views of the capital.

## Hilton Abu Dhabi

PO Box 877, Abu Dhabi, UAE
Tel: (+971 2) 692 4123, fax: (+971 2) 681 1696
e-mail: auhhitwrm@hilton.com   www.hilton.com

The Hilton Abu Dhabi enjoys an envious setting on the island city's beautiful Corniche, where it overlooks the Arabian Gulf. It is also conveniently located just a short drive from downtown Abu Dhabi, two minutes away from the all-new Marina Shopping Mall at the breakwater and just 30 minutes drive from the International Airport. The hotel offers 350 deluxe rooms and facilities and thematic restaurants and bars to suit the different needs of different clients. Hilton guests can also avail themselves of a fully equipped gym and relax at the Hiltonia Beach Club.

## Hilton Al Ain

PO Box 1333, Al Ain, UAE
Tel: (+971 3) 768 6666, fax: (+971 3) 768 7597
e-mail: RM_AL-AIN@hilton.com   www.hilton.com

The Hilton Al Ain is located close to the heart of the Oasis City. A luxurious selection of rooms, suites and chalets make up its 202 rooms while the award-winning culinary team spoils you in the Casa Romana, Al Khayam Persian, Jahili, Paco's, Hiltonia and Peach Garden restaurants and clubs. Perfectly located for meetings and seminars, the hotel offers fully-equipped rooms for six to 600 participants. The Hiltonia club has state of the art facilities, with the only green-grass, nine-hole golf course in Al Ain and a full complement of other facilities. For business or leisure Hilton Al Ain, offers it all.

## InterContinental – Abu Dhabi

PO Box 4171, Abu Dhabi, UAE
Tel: (+971 2) 666 6888, fax: (+971 2) 666 1388
e-mail: auhha-reservation@interconti.com   www.intercontinental.com

The InterContinental is situated in a parkland setting on a private beach. Overlooking a palm-studded island and the Presidential Palace, the hotel is close to diplomatic and government quarters and five minutes from the city centre. The 330 bedrooms have spectacular views of the Gulf and city skyline. Club Intercontinental is a whole floor dedicated to executives and the hotel's conference and banqueting facilities are said to be the finest in the country. The Inter-fitness health club is the leading recreation facility in the city, while the hotel is a paradise for water-sports enthusiasts and sun worshippers – the private beaches being an absolute delight.

## InterContinental Resort Al Ain

PO Box 16031, Al Ain, UAE
Tel: (+971 3) 768 6686, fax: (+971 3) 768 6162
e-mail: alain@interconti.com   www.intercontinental.com

For business or pleasure, the InterContinental Resort – Al Ain is the ideal destination for relaxation and fun. Excellent leisure facilities, including a childrens' playground and a wide range of sporting and adventure pursuits, provide something for everyone. The resort is located in the Oasis City, just 90 minutes drive from both Abu Dhabi and Dubai. The 216 well-appointed rooms and suites are fully air-conditioned and all have a balcony. In addition, 22 Mediterranean-style villas provide families, weekenders and business executives with a choice of elegant accommodation, while a diverse range of restaurants and bars take guests on a culinary journey around the world.

## Grand Continental Flamingo Hotel

PO Box 28080, Abu Dhabi, UAE
Tel: (+971 2) 626 2200, fax: (+971 2) 626 4333
e-mail: grndconh@emirates.net.ae

Abu Dhabi's only 'boutique hotel' has 152 elegantly-furnished rooms and suites that are spacious and provide stunning views of the Gulf and Khalifa Gardens. All are air-conditioned, with mini-bars, satellite TV, IDD telephones and 24-hour room service and the Executive suites each have their own kitchenette. The 'Flamingo Club Rooms' have data ports for direct laptop connection and other business facilities, and non-smoking rooms are available. You can enjoy a daily international buffet in Bistro Med, genuine Italian cuisine in award-winning Peppino, traditional English pub grub in Sherlock's or an exclusive range of beverages in the Clansman Lounge.

## Le Meridien Abu Dhabi

PO Box 46066, Abu Dhabi, UAE
Tel: (+971 2) 644 6666, fax: (+971 2) 644 0348
e-mail: meridien@emirates.net.ae   www.lemeridien-abudhabi.com

Set in beautiful gardens overlooking the Gulf, this five-star beach-front property provides a vast spectrum of services, with 15 enticing outlets offering international and oriental cuisine. There's also the newly refurbished Royal Club executive floor, a business
centre, superb conference and banqueting facilities, a health spa and recreational facilities. The hotel features 159 standard rooms, 46 Royal Club, a Royal Club lounge and
21 suites. In addition, a residence area offers studios and suites overlooking the sea. Le
Meridien Abu Dhabi, the most central and well-located hotel in the capital, provides
the perfect setting for an idyllic vacation or a stress-free business visit.

## Millennium Hotel Abu Dhabi

PO Box 44486, Abu Dhabi, UAE
Tel: (+971 2) 626 2700, fax: (+971 2) 626 0333
e-mail: sales.abudhabi@mill.cop.com  www.millenniumhotels.com

Standing on Khalifa Street, the Millennium Hotel Abu Dhabi makes its mark as the
capital's newest five-star business-lifestyle hotel. With guest facilities including 325 luxurious guestrooms, a magnificent Grand Ballroom and a diverse range of culinary
options, the hotel caters perfectly for both corporate and leisure travellers. With a striking mix of understated Arabian and contemporary styles, guests are assured of refined
service and impeccable Middle Eastern hospitality. The Millennium Hotel Abu Dhabi
is operated by Millennium Hotels and Resorts, a global hotel company with a portfolio
of 91 hotels in 17 countries worldwide.

## Sands Hotel Abu Dhabi

PO Box 32430, Abu Dhabi, UAE
Tel: (+971 2) 633 5335, fax: (+971 2) 633 5766
e-mail: sandshot@emirates.net.ae  www.sands-hotel.com

The Sands Hotel Abu Dhabi, the best-value five-star deluxe hotel in the city, is cen-
trally located in the heart of the capital, close to commercial and business districts,
government offices and embassies and within walking distance of major shopping
centres. The property has 253 spacious rooms and suites, including an Amiri Suite and
Club Sands – two executive floors with 60 rooms and suites along with a fully equipped
Executive Club Lounge. For dining there's a choice of six different styles of restaurant
offering a wide range of cuisine from Chinese to Lebanese, Mediterranean, Italian and
International – enough to suit all tastes.

## Sheraton Abu Dhabi Resort & Towers

PO Box 640, Abu Dhabi, UAE
Tel: (+971 2) 677 3333, fax: (+971 2) 672 5149
e-mail: sheraton@emirates.net.ae  www.sheraton.com

Situated on the Corniche, within walking distance of the shopping and commercial
districts and just 30 minutes' drive from the airport, the hotel has 273 deluxe rooms
including three executive floors and 17 suites. The new Palms Beach Resort with its
pools and a fully-equipped health club is surrounded by a private beach. A variety of
stylish restaurants provide an international dining experience, including Italian,
Mexican and seafood; while you can enjoy a drink at Silk Road, the Tavern, Tapas Bar
Bravo or the elegant Cigar Bar & Bottle Club. There's also a business centre, six conference and meeting rooms and an open-air amphitheatre.

# Acknowledgements

The publishers would like to thank HH Sheikh Nahayan bin Mabarak Al Nahayan, UAE Minister of Higher Education and Scientific Research, for providing the introduction to this book and the Ministry of Information and Culture in Abu Dhabi for checking page proofs.

We would also like to thank the following organisations for supplying us with photographs from their private libraries and archives: Abu Dhabi Company for Onshore Oil Operations (Adco), Abu Dhabi Duty Free, Abu Dhabi Golf Club by Sheraton, Abu Dhabi International Airport, Abu Dhabi National Oil Company (Adnoc), British Petroleum, Gulf Aircraft Maintenance Company (Gamco), Mina Zayed, Ministry of Information, Sharjah Commerce & Tourism Development Authority, Sunshine Tours, The Gulf Centre for Remote Sensing, TotalFinaElf and Victory Team.

# Photographic Credits

| | |
|---|---|
| Abu Dhabi Duty Free | 94, 96/97 |
| Abu Dhabi Golf Club by Sheraton | 83B |
| Abu Dhabi International Airport | 51 |
| Adco | 3, 8, 21, 22, 23 |
| Adnoc | 58, 59 |
| Al Blankli, Arif | 37T |
| Aspinall, Simon | 75T, 75B |
| Bird, James | 88T |
| British Petroleum | 56 |
| Codrai, Ronald | 52/53 |
| Crowell, Charles | 34T, 34B, 40, 55, 64/65 |
| Ferrari, Jorge | 10, 24/25 |
| Gulf Air | 48 |
| Gulf Aircraft Maintenance Company (Gamco) | 49 |
| Hellyer, Peter | 32T, 54 |
| Jebreili, Kamran | 32B |
| Krämer, Eva | 37B, 62 |
| Mellor, Chris | Front cover, 9, 31B, 33, 90B |
| Mina Zayed | 50 |
| Ministry of Information | 19 |
| Motivate Publishing: Shankar, Adiseshan: | Title page, 6/7, 11, 12/13, 14/15, 28, 29T, 29B, 30/31, 38/39, 41, 43, 44, 45, 46, 47, 61, 65, 66T, 66B, 67T, 67B, 68, 69T, 69B, 70/71, 71R, 72T, 76/77, 77, 78, 80B, 86/87, 88B, 89T, 89B, 90T, 91, 92, 93, 94/95, 98, back cover |
| Rashid, Noor Ali | 16/17, 20 |
| Robinson, Dave | 74 |
| Photodisc | 83 |
| Steele, David | 63 |
| Sunshine Tours | 84T, 85 |
| The Gulf Centre for Remote Sensing | 26/27 |
| TotalFinaElf | 56/57 |
| Victory Team/Ferrari, Jorge | 79 |
| Zandi, Daruish | 35, 60, 72/73, 82, 97T |

Abbreviations: T=top; B=Bottom; L=Left; R=Right

# THE ARABIAN HERITAGE SERIES

*If you've enjoyed this book you might like to read some of the other Motivate titles.*

*Further titles are available. For more information visit our website:*

**booksarabia.com**